An ABC of Queen Victoria's Empire

An ABC of Queen Victoria's Empire

Or a Primer of Conquest, Dissent and Disruption

Antoinette Burton

With contributions by Zarena Aslami,
Tracey Banivanua Mar, Tony Ballantyne, Bridget Brereton,
Adele Perry, T. J. Tallie and Irina Spector-Marks

Bloomsbury Academic
An imprint of Bloomsbury Publishing Plc

B L O O M S B U R Y
LONDON · OXFORD · NEW YORK · NEW DELHI · SYDNEY

Bloomsbury Academic

An imprint of Bloomsbury Publishing Plc

50 Bedford Square
London
WC1B 3DP
UK

1385 Broadway
New York
NY 10018
USA

www.bloomsbury.com

BLOOMSBURY and the Diana logo are trademarks of Bloomsbury Publishing Plc

First published 2017

British Library Cataloguing-in-Publication Data

A catalogue record for this book is available from the British Library.

ISBN: HB: 978-1-4742-3015-5
       PB: 978-1-4742-3016-2
       ePDF: 978-1-4742-3018-6
       ePub: 978-1-4742-3017-9

Library of Congress Cataloging-in-Publication Data

Names: Burton, Antoinette M., 1961– author.
Title: An ABC of Queen Victoria's empire : or a primer of conquest, dissent and disruption / Antoinette Burton.
Description: London ; New York : Bloomsbury Academic, 2017.
Identifiers: LCCN 2016025095 | ISBN 9781474230155 (hardback) | ISBN 9781474230162 (paperback)
Subjects: LCSH: Great Britain—History—Victoria, 1837–1901—Historiography. | Great Britain—Colonies—History—19th century. | Imperialism—Government policy—Great Britain. | Imperialism—History—19th century. | BISAC: HISTORY / World. | HISTORY / Modern / 19th Century. | HISTORY / Modern / 20th Century.
Classification: LCC DA551 .B87 2017 | DDC 909.0971/2081—dc23
LC record available at https://lccn.loc.gov/2016025095

Cover design: Sharon Mah
Cover image: Attack on the Court-House, St. Thomas-in-the-East, Jamaica, during Morant Bay Rebellion, 11 October 1865 © Photo by Culture Club/Getty Images

Typeset by RefineCatch Limited, Bungay, Suffolk
Printed and bound in India

*The best way of imparting theoretical instruction [is] to give it out
in short installments with ample illustrative examples* ...
—ROBERT BADEN-POWELL, *SCOUTING FOR BOYS* (1908)

For David Francis Burton
and his loving mother

Contents

List of Images

6   Famine 42

"Praying to Nandi for relief from Famine, Bengal, India, 1874."
From *The Illustrated London News*, London, February 21, 1874,
Getty Images.

7   Gandhi, Mohandas K. 47

"Indian lawyer, activist and statesman Mohandas Karamchand
Gandhi (1869–1948) recuperating after being severely beaten on
10th February." Dinodia Photos, Getty Images.

8   Hosay 52

"Postcard showing tadjahs (tazias) made for the Hosay
(Muharram) festival, Trinidad, c. 1912." 43C, Folder 14, Box 7 of
Goldberg Collection, The Alma Jordan Library, The University
of the West Indies, St. Augustine, Republic of Trinidad and
Tobago.

9   Indenture 57

"Group of Indian coolies, South Africa, c. 1890. From a series of
lantern slides on the South African diamond and gold mines."
Print Collector, Getty Images.

10 Jihad 63

"Preaching 'Holy War' during an uprising in British India, 1897,
artist F. Meaulle, *Le Petit Journal*, October 3, 1897." Print
Collector, Getty Images.

11 Kīngitanga 68

"Tawhiao I (1822–1894) the Maori king of New Zealand, leader
of the Wiakato tribes. Tawhiao has the fine facial tattooing of the
high-ranking Maori." Getty Images.

Acknowledgments

Historians today are being asked to think about a variety of ways of helping students of the past engage with its facts and fictions beyond the scholarly monograph. This little book is one attempt to do just that. While I could not have conceived of or written it—or reached out to draw on the expertise of my co-contributors—without years of conventional research and writing, I recognize the necessity, indeed the urgency, of imagining alternative forms of historical thinking and presentation. I hope this *ABC* moves conversations about form and content forward in the field of British Empire history. I hope, too, that those who pick it up will pursue further primary research and/or secondary reading beyond the initial entries so that they can have a fuller understanding of how imperialism worked, how it didn't, and who and what shaped it—not just affirmatively, but via dissent and disruption as well.

I am grateful to several people who helped me think through this idea and do some of the research that undergirds it. Zack Poppel spent hours combing the Getty Archive for appropriate images. He was and remains a valuable interlocutor and colleague. Scott Harrison accepted a grand out-of-field research challenge in the summer of 2015, and the results have gone a long way toward underwriting this book. Thanks to him for his intellectual energy and unwavering commitment to feminist and antiracist histories. Utathya Chattopadhyaya also provided critical guidance and shared some of his own work, which was invaluable. Emily Pope-Obeda was essential in the final stages, balancing her own research and writing with the exigencies of primer design and delivery at a busy time, for which I am very appreciative. Isabel Hofmeyr is the best reader I know, and the eye she cast on the book at various stages really helped me move it along. Last but not least, participants in the History Workshop at the University of Illinois challenged me to think in broad strokes and deep detail about what the book could and should do. I am especially grateful to Marc Hertzman for hugely helpful feedback, to Terri Barnes for helping me think through the indigenous language question and to Ken Cuno for saving me from some infelicitous factual errors. My colleagues at Illinois, past and present, are always my first and best readers.

At Bloomsbury, Claire Lipscomb has been a fully engaged editor from the moment we met that day at the Bedford Square offices. She has a genuine interest in the books she commissions and she has been uncommonly enthusiastic about this project. Emma Goode has a lot of patience on many fronts, and I appreciate all she has done to keep the production part moving. Thanks to the Bastian fund and to the History department, the College of Liberal Arts and Sciences, and the Office of the Vice Chancellor for Research at the University of Illinois for affording me the resources to bring the project to fruition. Tom Bedwell's work on behalf of many historians I know is a true gift. Thanks as well to Paul, Nick and Olivia for putting up with my creative jags, which have a tendency to interrupt the circadian rhythms of our household.

Last but not least, Zarena, Tony, Tracey, Bridget, Adele, Irina and T. J. took time from their busy lives to carve out some key "letters" for this project. Without them, the arc of *A* to *Z* would not have been possible. Their contributions, as well as the labors of Zack, Scott, Utathya and Emily, are a testimony to the ways that all challenging histories are usually the work of many hands. It's now up to students to make their own ABCs of empire in reply.

Notes on Contributors

Zarena Aslami (Y is for Yakub Khan) is an Associate Professor in the Department of English at Michigan State University and the author of *The Dream Life of Citizens: Late Victorian Novels and the Fantasy of the State*. She is currently working on a book about Victorian representations of Afghanistan, and in particular, their construction of and fascination with the problem of Afghan political authority.

Tony Ballantyne (K is for Kīngitanga) is the Director of the Centre for Research on Colonial Culture at the University of Otago, where he also serves as Pro-Vice-Chancellor Humanities. He has published widely on the culture of British empire-building and his most recent book is *Entanglements of Empire: Missionaries, Māori, and the Question of the Body* (Duke University Press and Auckland University Press).

Tracey Banivanua Mar (Q is for Queensland Sugar) is an Australian Research Council Future Fellow at La Trobe University who studies colonial, imperial and indigenous histories in the interconnected worlds of the Pacific and Pacific Rim. She is the author of *Violence and Colonial Dialogue: The Australian-Pacific Indentured Labour Trade* (University of Hawaii Press, 2007), *Decolonisation and the Pacific: Indigenous Globalisation and the Ends of Empire* (2016) and co-editor with Penny Edmonds of *Making Settler Colonial*

Space: Perspectives on Race, Place and Identity (Palgrave
Macmillan, 2010).

Bridget Brereton (H is for Hosay) is Emerita Professor of History at
UWI, St. Augustine, Trinidad and Tobago. She is the author of
several books on the history of the Caribbean and of Trinidad,
including standard works such as *Race Relations in Colonial
Trinidad, 1870–1900* and *A History of Modern Trinidad, 1783–1962.*
She is the editor or co-editor of several more (including Volume V of
the UNESCO General History of the Caribbean), and the author of
many journal articles, book chapters and book reviews.

Antoinette Burton (editor and author of A–G, J, L–P, S–W and Z)
is Professor of History and Bastian Professor of Global and
Transnational Studies at the University of Illinois, Urbana-Champaign.
Her most recent books are *The Trouble with Empire: Challenges to
Modern British Imperialism* (Oxford, 2015), and co-edited with Dane
Kennedy, *How Empire Shaped Us* (Bloomsbury, 2016).

Adele Perry (R is for Riel, Louis) teaches history at the University of
Manitoba, where she gets a day off in February in honor of Louis
Riel. Perry has worked on Canadian history, women's and gender
history and comparative colonial histories, and is the author, most
recently, of *Colonial Relations: The Douglas-Connolly Family and the
Nineteenth-Century Imperial World* (Cambridge, 2015).

Irina Spector-Marks (I is for Indenture) is a graduate student in the
Department of History at the University of Illinois, at Urbana-
Champaign. Research interests include diaspora and migration, print
culture, and Indian Ocean and British Empire history. Her
dissertation, "Circuits of Imperial Citizenship: Indian Print Culture
and the Politics of Race, 1890–1914," examines the transnational
political trajectories and racialized meanings of Indian imperial
citizenship at the turn of the twentieth century. Publications appear

or are forthcoming in the *Journal of Colonialism and Colonial History* and *Charting Imperial Itineraries: Unmooring the Komagata Maru*, edited by Satwinder Kaur Bains, Davina Bhandar, Rita Kaur Dhamoon and Renisa Mawani.

T. J. Tallie (X is for Xhosaland) is an Assistant Professor of African History at Washington and Lee University. His work focuses on indigeneity, race, gender and settler colonialism. He is at work on his book manuscript titled *Unsettling Natal: Race, Gender, and Colonial Logics in Southern Africa, 1850–1910.*

in the 1890s as part of a lantern slide show series, is staged to create a picturesque scene that masks the terrible conditions under which most "coolies" labored.

(p. 68) K is for Kingitanga: *Tawhiao I (1822-1894) the Maori king of New Zealand, leader of the Wiakato tribes. Tawhiao has the fine facial tattooing of the high-ranking Maori.*

(p. 57) I is for Indenture: *Indenture was a brutal labor regime that took many forms across the British Empire in the nineteenth century. This picture, taken in South Africa ... to underscore a familial ... Indenture was a brutal labor regime that took many forms*

Bloomsbury ...

Bloomsbury regrets the presence of two erroneous images on pages 57 and 68; the correct images with their accompanying captions are presented below.

(p. 57) I is for Indenture: *Indenture was a brutal labor regime that took many forms across the British Empire in the nineteenth century. This picture, taken in South Africa in the 1890s as part of a lantern slide show series, is staged to underscore a familial scene that masks the terrible conditions under which most "coolies" labored.*

(p. 68) K is for Kīngitanga: *Tawhiao I (1822-1894) the Maori king of New Zealand, leader of the Wiakato tribes. Tawhiao has the fine facial tattooing of the high-ranking Maori.*

child as a community member as well. Even when images graced alphabet primers in the early nineteenth century, the singularity of the letter linked the message of discipline and order and good self-government to the singularity of the individual child. Such attributes might be as easily cultivated by the bad example ("Z was a Zany that did not Love Learning") as by good ("Y was a Youth that Had Great Discerning"). This pair rounded out the 1822 book *The Alphabet Ladder* with just such comparative pedagogy. In this particular alphabet environment, the point was not just the act of reading the alphabet, but also the process of internalizing the moral lessons it instilled.[3]

In Victorian Britain, the links between the ABC and the nexus of capitalism and empire were key to the ideological work of Ames's book. As the discourse of economic exchange became the discourse of social exchange in the context of the industrial revolution, the emphasis was increasingly on the cultivation of children as consumers and on their self-understanding as members of a marketized imperial nation.[4] And as commodification reached further and further into private life, the ABC concept became part of an industry of pedagogy, from toys to books to *Boys' Own* adventure material—culminating by 1908 in that *summa cum laude* of imperial primers, Robert Baden-Powell's *Scouting for Boys*.[5] In this developmental reading landscape, the alphabet became a conveyance as well as a commodity.[6] It was a means of bringing distant objects close for incipient readers, and in the case of *An ABC for Baby Patriots*, of delivering imperial people, places and ambitions into the hands of parents and children who reached for Mrs. Ames's compact storybook.

Mrs. Ames supplied a range of entertaining images to match her capital letters and confident texts. In "B is for Battle," the accompanying illustration evoked "national" monuments such as the ones in Trafalgar Square as imperial archives, with the list of wars (India, China, Egypt,

Khartoum) inscribed at the base. "C is for Colonies" represented an Englishman in what looks like a gold-miner's hat being fanned by a dark-skinned, vaguely oriental servant—bringing empire and its status complexities directly to the reader's attention. "I is for India" reprises the fanning theme, but the Englishman being cooled is holding a gun while sitting atop an elephant, aiming languidly at a lion and a tiger below him. *O* evokes *Rule Britannia* via "the Ocean/ where none but a fool/Would ever dare question/our title to rule." And as indicated above, *Z* ends triumphantly—complete with father and children marching around the nursery in mock parade while carrying the Union Jack.

In Ames's fin de siècle alphabet plot, gender is key to how the reader is oriented vis-à-vis the objects of empire. The cover depicts a blond girl astride a horse, saluting a toy soldier. She is clearly mimicking the posture and ceremonial function of the Queen, who naturally gets her own letter ("Q is for Queen!/it fills us with pride/To see the Queen's coach/When the Queen is inside"). The girl also appears, staring at a globe with an insouciant, possessive look, sword at her side, in "E is our Empire/Where the sun never sets." ("The larger we make it/The Bigger it gets.") But beyond that, and unsurprisingly, this is the story of men. *H* (Hunting), *P* (Parliament) *T* (the Englishman's Tub!), *D* (Daring) and *G* (Game)—all these evoke stereotypically upper-class or aspirationally middle-class Victorian modes of racialized masculinity. In most cases, whiteness is unmarked: The presumptive site of male privilege is so natural that it need not speak its name. An instructive exception is *K* (for Kings): "Once warlike and haughty/ Great Britain subdued them/Because they'd been naughty." The image is of robed and booted white men dragging two shoeless Africanized potentates, one of whom has a decidedly simian look, behind them in chains. The contrast of this scene of abjection with the invocation of childlike "naughtiness" in the rhyme is arresting, a reminder that

Victorian childhood was by no means innocent of the psychic imprint of empire and its racism, which was as casual as it was deeply embedded. Meanwhile, it's hard not see echoes of the 1879 Zulu War, and the defeat and capture of Cetshwayo KaMpande (c. 1826–1884), the Zulu monarch, in this particular figuration. That echo makes Mrs. Ames's alphabet a delivery system for late Victorian history as well as a species of *Boys' Own* adventure fiction. Or her primer is an avatar of that genre: It is an embryonic precursor, a teaser for the world of imperial *bildungsromans* to come for the lifelong imperial reader.

Its silly and playful tone notwithstanding, *An ABC for Baby Patriots* was deadly serious. It took its place alongside a host of primers, many of them written by women who raced to keep up with both the expanding empire and the market for pedagogical tools designed to help students apprehend Britain's global expansion and influence. The vast majority of these were geographical texts written for school-age children. Like Mary Anne Venning's popular book, *The Geographical Present*, they might deliver knowledge about policy and ideas in a systematized way; or like Barbara Hofland's *The Panorama of Europe*, they might cast the lesson as a game. Taken together, the imperial ABC and the geography primer mapped "the spatial forms and fantasies through which a culture declares its presence."[7] And by bringing images and doggerel about Britain's imperial culture into the nursery and the parlor, Mrs. Ames helped close the gap between home and away, and nurture children's understanding that empire belonged to them as late Victorians on the verge of a new century. Like many of her fellow women writers for children, she was invested in promoting early convictions about the favorableness of British rule.[8]

Despite its ostensible target audience, Mrs. Ames's *ABC* has more rather than less in common with the wide variety of "abecedariums" that populated the landscape of Victorian scientific and semi-scientific literature. A quick glance at the online British Library catalogue reveals a raft of Victorian alphabet books, cataloguing everything from phrenology to quadrupeds to animals to nations to Irish policy to economic science to insects to beasts to "common objects" to alphabets themselves. This range of primers suggests that the Victorian ABC was a classificatory system as well as an orientation device—more secular (and physically flexible) than a hornbook and more directional than a sampler. From the 1880s on, when print culture took off in unprecedented ways, the ABC was arguably a newly effective winnowing tool, instrumental for managing the vast amounts of information now available to a certain class of readers who might never hope for mastery, but might still aspire to a degree of encyclopedic knowledge, pointedly alphabetized.

The ABC also held out the possibility of introductory, elementary knowledge: Whether aimed at children or not, it was an invitation to the nonspecialist to enter into a foreign or inaccessible subject in a very basic way, though its pedagogical techniques could be quite sophisticated. Its association with childhood and with innocence might license a sense of "sentimental possession" at once individual and collective.[9] The ABC form gives the impression, in other words, that all subjects are knowable through English nursery rhyme instruction. In a nineteenth-century liberalizing context, it appears to be an instrument of developmental democratic learning. In the context of the late nineteenth-century imperial nation-state, it offers the promise of global-imperial belonging that is as effortless as *ABC*. In Mrs. Ames's primer, the pedagogy of alphabetization is linked to the making of an imperial self through the eyes of a child, who in turn imagines a world manifestly driven by guns and white male power to which everyone else is either happily or despondently subject. It narrates the beginning and end of that promise and enables readers to think of themselves as confident consumers of all things imperial, from *A* to *Z*.

To be sure, such a self-serious genre had its playful interlocutors. Walter Crane, the socialist illustrator and one of the most important children's book creators of the Victorian period, produced *The Absurd ABC* in 1874.[10] Dedicated as he was to thinking through the relationship between design and the process of reading, he arguably sidelined the letters themselves and placed much more emphasis visually on the link between the illustration for each entry and the ditty that accompanied it. Out of the eight pages that comprised the alphabet book, five scattered the letters across the entire page, which means that the reader is connecting the text with the image rather than with A or B per se. The absurdity consists in the shambolic nature of the alphabetization as well as in the whimsical rhymes ("T stand for Tom/the son of the piper/May his principles change/as his years go riper"). At the same time, *The Absurd ABC* is a paean to an Anglo-Saxon folktale tradition, right down to the Q for Queen Anne and E for the Englishman in *Jack and the Beanstalk*. Empire or a critique of it is nowhere to be seen here. That is not because Crane was uninterested in imperialism. One of the most iconically imperial maps of the period—the Imperial Federation League Map of 1886—has been recently attributed to him. But the vision of empire it realizes, while imaginative and eye-catching, points to a socialist aesthetic practice that centered labor without subverting empire. The same may be said of his *Absurd ABC*, which to echo Felix Driver, performs an unproblematic insular Englishness rather than critiquing it.[11]

So, Victorian ABCs could be send-ups, but this was rare enough. Meanwhile, if Mrs. Ames's *ABC* was an imperial orientation device, ours should be thought of as an anti-imperial *re*-orientation device, one that queers the genre—not by upending it through simple reversals, but by detaching it from its familiar moorings through a re-appropriation of its basic principle, alphabetization, and a parody of its pro-empire intentions.[12] We use the alphabet form to narrate not the extension and hegemony of a metro-centric empire, but rather, to rematerialize the forces and figures who challenged its presumption or threw it on the defense or revealed the inconvenient truths about the racialized and sexualized violences that enabled it—both at home and in the colonies. "A is for the Afghan Wars," "J is for Jihad," "O is for Opium," "X is for Xhosaland"—this is not your grandmother's glorious empire story. Each letter hails a history of struggle, subjection, resistance and/or dissent in order to signal that the terrain of Victorian imperialism was not linear or progressive, but full of fault-lines and frictions every step of the way. Readers take note: In keeping with the spirit of Mrs. Ames's primer, this is an ABC of the *Victorian* imperial project. Many of the entries tag events or people whose influence was felt well beyond the nineteenth century: Gandhi and Churchill come most obviously to mind, as do jihad and syphilis. But we focus here on the pre-1901 histories that attach to each letter. On the premise that the Victorian period sponsored some of the most lingering forms and aspects of modern imperialism in its twentieth- and twenty-first-century iterations, at least in the anglophone world, this nineteenth-century focus is warranted.

Our *ABC* recodes Victoria's empire, therefore, as troublesome and dissident and disruptive, dramatizing how and why rebels and insurgents and enemies of imperialism thwarted the Pax Britannica for which the nineteenth century is considered uniquely famous.[13] That narrative of the "savage wars of peace" continues to shape apprehensions of British imperialism in the contemporary present in ways that not only distort its histories, but also defer crucial questions about the continuities of anglo-imperial power in the twenty-first-century world. If we understand the two Victorian campaigns in Afghanistan as central to the story of modern British imperialism, rather than peripheral to it, for example, do we not need to rethink the origins and meanings of recent global events in that region? If we recognize famine as state failure across several imperial sites, do we not appreciate with greater analytical insight the legacies of empire for global hunger today? And if we know that syphilis was a major source of anxiety for Victorian imperial officials, to such a degree that they openly debated its role in the social and sexual disorder of colonial possessions, are we not obligated to think through similar questions about today's military management of gender difference and the role of prostitution and rape in neo-imperial war? The ABC is a deceptively simple genre indeed.

All of this begs an equally pressing question: To what extent can we really subvert the ABC when we are working so thoroughly inside the form? Each letter serves as an occasion for elaborating *both* a history of coercion and/or dissent *and* a set of linked references that make connections between and among entries. So, we note that Gandhi and Churchill are from the same generation; that jihad circulates from India to Afghanistan and back again; that Urabi's revolution had much in common with other forms of native claim-making; that bold Fenian men and convict women make an interesting juxtaposition. Just as imperial spaces and people and ideas were interdependent, then, no letter is sovereign; each one leaks and bleeds into related terrains, showing up empire to be more than simply colonizer and colonized, home and away, the Raj or the white settler colony. As such, our anti-imperial alphabet serves readers as a citationary apparatus. It allows them to read about trans- and inter-colonial histories: to consider empire's dispersal as well as its consolidation, and the tension between the two. If Victorian ABC books were implicitly celebratory of the subjects they catalogued, our *ABC* is decidedly not. We don't hold up imperialism to classificatory wonder; we challenge readers to understand the many ways in which it was violent and turbulent on the ground, its territorial ambitions challenged and its hegemony interrupted, if not thwarted entirely.

Would Victorian readers have been shocked? Perhaps. And yet, as so many of the entries here show, scenes of dissent and disruption made their way into newspapers, memoirs and political accounts of the time. Nineteenth-century reading audiences, at any rate, were well aware of the recurrence of war and rebellion and jihad. Did they find these elements gathered all in one place? No. Knowledge about challenges to imperialism was as dispersed as the empire itself, and no contemporary ABC did the work of making it visible between two covers. Our *ABC* has the benefit of distance and critical perspective: one advantage of the historian. Taken together, the letters that make up this primer not only catalog a number of consequential challenges to imperial power, they also attempt to map a counter-history of Victorian narratives of Pax Britannica that winnowed out the dynamics of coercion and resistance to hegemony on the ground. We need to move those tensions back to center stage in order more fully to appreciate how fundamental they were, and are, to how imperialism operates. Indeed, the ABCs of empire are not complete without them.

There are many ways to learn and think, and to read and write and teach, about British imperialism (see "How to Teach this Book," p. 153). This *ABC* is not intended as a substitute for more in-depth studies of the Raj, of indigenous resistance or of the working of race and sexuality in the empire. Like its predecessors, perhaps, it is deceptively simple, even perversely playful. Start at the beginning and read all the way through. Pick a letter at random and follow the internal citations until you've woven your way from *S* to *L* and back again. Use the list of suggested alternatives at the end of each entry ("A is also for . . .") to develop your own counter-ABC. Track down a suggested reading or two to deepen your knowledge of *X*, *Y* or *Z*. No matter what your approach, remember that once you know your ABCs, you realize that they are profoundly disorienting, in the best possible ways. And then the fun—or is it the work?—really begins.[14]

Notes

1 Mrs. Ernest Ames, *An ABC for Baby Patriots* (London: Dean and Son, Ltd., 1899). For a link to the book see: http://digilib.usm.edu/cdm/ref/collection/dgbooks/id/2738. Last accessed February 2, 2016.

2 Patricia Crain, *The Story of A: The Alphabetization of America from the New England Primer to the Scarlett Letter* (Palo Alto: Stanford University Press, 2000), 65–68.

3 Crain, *The Story of A*, 75, 88.

4 Denise Denisoff, "Small Change: The Consumerist Designs of the Nineteenth-Century Child" in her edited collection, *The Nineteenth Century Child and Consumer Culture* (Surrey: Ashgate, 2008), 7–12.

5 Elleke Boehmer, ed., *Scouting for Boys: The Original 1908 Edition* (Oxford University Press, 2005) and her essay, "The Text in the World, the World through the Text: Robert Baden-Powell's *Scouting for Boys*" in Antoinette Burton and Isabel Hofmeyr, eds, *Ten Books that Shaped the British Empire: Creating an Imperial Commons* (Durham: Duke University Press, 2014), 131–152.

6 Crain, *The Story of A*, 99.

7 Megan N. Norcia, *X Marks the Spot: Women Writers Map the Empire for British Children, 1790–1895* (Athens: Ohio University Press, 2010), 5, 19, 34, 44.

8 Norcia, *X Marks the Spot*, 61.

9 Crain, *The Story of A.*, 155.

10 Walter Crane, *The Absurd ABC* (London: G. Routledge, 1874). See also Isobel Spenser, *Walter Crane* (New York: Macmillan, 1975), where she comments on its "rollicking mood" (60).

11 Felix Driver, "In Search of the Imperial Map: Walter Crane and the Image of Empire," *History Workshop Journal* 69 (2010): 156.

12 See Sara Ahmed, *Queer Phenomenology: Orientations, Objects, Others* (Durham: Duke University Press, 2006) and Judith Butler, *Gender Trouble: Feminism and the Subversion of Identity* (London: Routledge, 1990).

13 Antoinette Burton, *The Trouble with Empire: Challenges to Modern British Imperialism* (Oxford: Oxford University Press, 2015).

The ABCs of
Victoria's Empire

A is for the Afghan Wars

This most dramatic of images renders the capture that led to the assassination of William MacNaghten, British political agent in Afghanistan, at the hands of Dost Mohammed in 1841. His death fed narratives of Afghan savagery and English martyrdom. Print Collector, Hulton Archive.

Despite the fact that Britain claimed victory in two wars in nineteenth-century Afghanistan, it is the specter of British failure in that country that persists today. Witnesses to the Victorian conflicts left account after account of how disastrously combat unfolded in difficult terrain in those campaigns (1839–1842 and 1878–1881). Indeed, the history of the first several Anglo-Afghan wars reads like a brief on the unruliness of the region and the limits of British military leadership in territory considered unmanageable because of snow and rough terrain. Early nineteenth-century military men were prolific about the challenges this frontier landscape posed to imperial ambition. But representations of the difficult terrain were arguably environmental fictions that allowed the British to downplay the threat posed by Afghan fighters. They blamed their limited success in subduing the region on a hostile environment—conflating insurgent landscapes with insurgent Afghans in the process. The idea that Afghanistan was ungovernable because of its challenging environment made it "the graveyard of empires" in the Victorian imagination.

In dispatches and briefs, military men warned that any invasion of Afghanistan by the Anglo-Indian army was doomed from the start. Official ideas about the impossibility of securing Afghanistan as a stronghold had less to do with British military capacity or the prospect of native resistance (see **J is for Jihad**) than with apprehensions about the terrain itself. The Duke of Wellington famously described the 1839 war as a "wild expedition into a distant region of rocks and deserts, of sands and ice and snow"—tantamount to folly and equivalent to "an act of infatuation." Montstuart Elphinstone, who brokered the very first diplomatic mission to Kabul, agreed: "If an army was sent up to the passes, and if we could feed it, no doubt we might take Cabul and set up [a rival king], but it was hopeless to maintain him in a poor, cold, strong and remote country, among so turbulent a people."

Elphinstone acknowledged the turbulent people, yet nineteenth-century accounts pay only scant attention to the legions of Afghan fighters who held their ground—thus, determining the outcome of battles large and small. This was infamously the case during the rout of 1842, when thousands of British troops, native bearers and camp followers were trapped and slaughtered in the "terrible defiles" between Kabul and Jellalabad. Novelist G. A. Henty attributed this darkest defeat to the fact that the Afghans were "dangerous among their mountains." Henty's two Afghan war novels, *To Herat and Cabul: A Story of the First Afghan War* (1901) and *For Name and Fame: Through Afghan Passes* (1902), helped to vivify the terror of the Afghan landscape and to popularize fantasies of Afghanistan as a treacherous and fatal battleground for readers well into the twentieth century. Although Henty does portray individual Afghan leaders as characters in these narratives, they stand out not for their military capability, but for their cunning and untrustworthiness. Henty was one of a number of contemporaries who relied on images of an alien environment to structure the narrative of British military debacle in Afghanistan and to sustain the fiction that the empire's greatest enemy was the inhospitable natural world (see **F is for Famine**).

Afghanistan was key to the strategic needs of a British imperial policy that saw India as its jewel in the crown and the settlement of its Northwest Frontier as critical to imperial security writ large. It also played a role in ideas about gender order in the imperial project. The ideal of the manly English soldier as the lord of all he surveyed has come down to us as the symbol of British imperial aspiration—the very stuff of boys' adventure fiction. That lively tradition of derring-do depended on ideas about "natural" mastery as the special virtue of Victorian imperialists. In 1839, British officers described tribal leaders as formidable opponents for whom they had reluctant respect. By 1879, however, these same men were seen as a different species: Beings whose capacity to blend into the local landscape called their very humanity into question. Images of Afghans as half-men, half-scorpions appear in both fiction and newspaper cartoons during the second campaign. This shift from Afghans as men to Afghans as semi-evolved creatures can be attributed to the impact of Darwinian racial thought and to the powerful resistance that well-organized forms of tribal leadership posed to Western ambition, especially by the time of the second campaign. Such representations relied equally on the absence of Afghan women from the drama of the Northwest Frontier. The second Afghan war ended (see **Y is for Yakub Khan**) with a settlement that the British brokered with the emir Abdur Rahman Kahn, whose tenure lasted until his death in 1901. His extended reign put paid to the notion that the empire had been bested by the environment rather than by an indigenous leader who could manage what the British, despite their claims to racial superiority and natural mastery, could not. Despite his success, the British dehumanized the Afghans and made conquest of the region equivalent to the takeover of an uninhabited landscape. In this scenario, local populations were effectively erased and Afghanistan was remarkable only for its perpetually ungovernable environment: an irresistible testing ground for British imperial claims to mastery of the natural world.

Victorians' anxieties about an inhospitable climate were not, of course, unfounded. Indeed, it proved fateful for more than just the officers, soldiers and camp followers of those nineteenth-century British wars. Referring to the doomed offensives of Anglo-American forces in the 2007 campaign in the Korengal Valley, war correspondent Sebastian Junger marveled that "it was as if every living thing in the valley, even the wildlife, wanted [us] gone" (*War*, 12). Junger's observation echoes a long history of narratives that have tried to explain Western failure in the region by assigning a major role to environmental factors in the making and unmaking of empire. No study of the wars can ignore the chokeholds that Afghanistan's terrain imposed on the paramount military force in the world at the time. The battle against the environment was not merely a natural fact, but also a convenient fiction that served to pardon British military failure in the region. The environmental fantasy that snow and impassable gorges were responsible for British short-comings shifted responsibility away from high command in London and Calcutta, and allowed policy-makers to ignore the tactical limitations of the Anglo-Indian army and the tenacity of Afghan resistance.

The two Anglo-Afghan campaigns of the Victorian period remind us that we should look more closely when failures of empire are attributed to the intransigence of the natural world or the incapacity of native people. Afghanistan's "natural" resistance to empire became an alibi for Britain's determination to occupy the region. Meanwhile, the Anglo-Afghan wars raise questions about the variety of fictions that have served as a rationales for expansion in other imperial locations as well.

Suggestions for Further Reading

Aslami, Zarena. "The Second Anglo-Afghan War, or The Return of the Uninvited." *BRANCH: Britain, Representation and Nineteenth-Century History*. Ed. Dino Franco Felluga. Extension of *Romanticism and Victorianism on the Net*. Last accessed November 2015.

Burton, Antoinette, ed. *The First Anglo-Afghan Wars: A Reader*. Durham: Duke University Press, 2014.

Dalrymple, William. *Return of a King: The Battle for Afghanistan, 1839–42*. New York: Vintage, 2014.

Henty, G. A. *To Herat and Cabul: A Story of the First Afghan War*. New York: Charles Scribner's and Sons, 1901.

Junger, Sebastian. *War*. New York: Hachette Book Group, 2011.

Schofield, Victoria. *Every Rock, Every Hill: The Plain Tale of the North-West Frontier and Afghanistan*. London: Buchan and Enright, 1984.

A is also for . . .

Aboriginal
Aden Settlement
Anglo-Boer War
Anglo-Maratha Wars
Anti-Chinese agitation
Ashanti

B

is for Bold Fenian Men

English-reading audiences were well aware of the disruption that Irish rebels caused at the heart of London in the mid-1860s. Here, The Penny Illustrated Paper reported the results of the Fenian bombing at Clerkenwell prison, where 12 people were killed and many more injured in an attempt to rescue Fenian prisoners. At five pence a copy, The Penny Illustrated was an affordable way of keeping up with weekly news from home and empire. Original publication: The Penny Illustrated Paper, 1867.

'Twas down by the glenside, I met an old woman
A-plucking young nettles, she ne'er saw me coming
I listened a while to the song she was humming
Glory O, Glory O, to the bold Fenian men.

'Tis fifty long years since I saw the moon beaming
On strong manly forms, on eyes with hope gleaming
I see them again, sure, in all my sad dreaming
Glory O, Glory O, to the bold Fenian men.

When I was a young girl, their marching and drilling
Awoke in the glenside sounds awesome and thrilling
They loved dear old Ireland, to die they were willing
Glory O, Glory O, to the bold Fenian men.

Some died by the glenside, some died near a stranger
And wise men have told us their cause was a failure
But they fought for old Ireland and never feared danger
Glory O, Glory O, to the bold Fenian men.

I passed on my way, God be praised that I met her
Be life long or short, sure I'll never forget her
We may have brave men, but we'll never have better
Glory O, Glory O, to the bold Fenian men.

Down by the Glenside, Peadar Kearney, c. 1916

Fenian was a watchword for rebellion and revolution across Victoria's empire. The Fenian movement was born of Irish grievances against English exploitation, an imperial relationship rooted, in turn, in the seventeenth-century Ulster plantation and nurtured by two centuries of aristocratic planter rule. But Fenianism was also a transnational phenomenon, extending from Dublin to Manchester to New York and Chicago and into Canada—linked by an Irish diaspora of republican thinkers and doers drawn from all walks of life. Fenians staged urban bombing campaigns and several outright "risings" in the nineteenth century. Though the latter were widely considered failures, they succeeded in bringing the specter of Irish violence to both the heart of the empire and to its outer reaches as well. The Fenians may not have used the word to describe their actions, but they made Irish republicanism synonymous with terror for many Victorians nonetheless.

The bold Fenians, memorialized in the twentieth-century song lyrics above, were marchers and drillers, to be sure, but they were idea men as well. They wanted self-government because they believed—fervently, even romantically—in the nation, a preoccupation they shared with many marginal communities in Europe and beyond who were subject to political exclusion in the nineteenth century. The revolution of 1848 catalyzed many such discontents in Europe. While Fenians were "men of 1848," they looked as much to the United States as to Europe. There, Irishmen such as John O'Mahony argued for revolution as the means to Irish independence from Britain and organized the Fenian Brotherhood in service to that end.

The Irish Republican Brotherhood (IRB), founded in Dublin a decade after the failures of 1848, was dedicated to the overthrow of British rule in Ireland. Its leaders created an international movement that included working-class Irish in the United States, Canada, and Australia as well as London and Glasgow. They staged uprisings in Canada in 1865 and Ireland in 1867, the same year that the Proclamation of the Irish Revolutionary Provisional Government was announced by "the Irish people to the world" (see **P is for the Proclamation of the Irish Republic**). A manifesto for equal rights and republican government, the Proclamation was also a declaration of war against British rule: "The soil of Ireland, at present in the possession of an oligarchy, belongs to us, the Irish people, and to us it must be restored" (*Chicago Tribune*, March 28, 1867, p. 2). The 1867 insurrection failed, but it produced mayhem and martyrs. Three IRB men were tried and publicly executed for their role in the "Manchester Outrages," an incident stemming from the escape attempts of Fenian prisoners that ended up killing a policeman. The Clerkenwell bombing later that year—which also involved a prisoner escape and ended up killing a dozen people—sealed the links between Fenianism and terror for many Victorians. "The Fenians have cast the glare of a great moral crime upon the debatable ground that separates us," wrote *The Times* of London. "We are confronted by a gang of criminals, who respect no law, human or divine ... we must crush them at any cost" (McCord in Harmon, *Fenians and Fenianism*, 48).

While 1867 was a failure, dynamite became a popular Fenian method. A dynamite campaign, orchestrated from the United States and targeting major cities in the United Kingdom, went on for the better part of 15 years. The IRB newspaper, *The Irish World*—which had subscribers in the tens of thousands—actively promoted it and received donations from all manner of readers who encouraged the Fenians to continue with their "missionary" work. Donovan O'Rossa, prominent IRB leader, was reported to have defended the dynamitard action unequivocally: "My motto is, strike away! Keep on striking till England is on her knees" (McKenna, 52). As the accompanying image suggests, contemporaries could see the damage right before their eyes.

The Fenians were a fraternal organization, but there were bold Fenian women as well. The Countess Markievicz and Maude Gonne were the most famous, but working-class Irish women sympathetic to the cause contributed in many ways. They marched in processions, provided meals and were encouraged from platforms by Fenian leaders to take up the patriotic labor required to sustain the movement. As one Fenian supporter remarked almost matter-of-factly, "There are enough Fenian women in New York to take the Canadas, if we wanted them" (Boulard, 57). Though many are nameless, women with Fenian connections and sympathies continued to do essential work for Irish independence into the twentieth century. The Ladies' Land Leaguers helped to train children in nationalist culture and sentiments; they were regular features at parades and picnics, and did their bit for fundraising as well (Praseta, 36–37). And as the lyrics to the song remind us, Irish women were the witness to and the historical memory for those Bold Fenian men, failures and all.

Suggestions for Further Reading

Boulard, Garry. *The Swing Around the Circle: Andrew Johnson and the Train Ride that Destroyed a Presidency*. iUniverse, 2008.

Harmon, Maurice, ed. *Fenians and Fenianism: Centenary Essays*. Seattle: University of Washington Press, 1970.

McKenna, Joseph. *The Irish-American Dynamite Campaign: A History, 1881–1896*. Jeffreson, NC: McFarland, 2012.

Praseta, Senia. *Irish Nationalist Women, 1900–1918*. Cambridge: Cambridge University Press, 2013.

Whelehan, Niall. *The Dynamiters: Irish Nationalism and Political Violence in the Wider World, 1867–1900*. Cambridge: Cambridge University Press, 2015.

B is also for . . .

Bambatha Rebellion
Berlin Conference
Boer
British Society for the Suppression of Opium
Bunyoro people

C is for Convict Women

Convict transportation involved a grim journey from the metropole to the Australian colonies. Though the emigrants pictured here traveled under less duress, they faced a long voyage and an uncertain future in the Antipodes as well. Hulton Archive, 1849.

In 1847, Caroline Chisholm, an English philanthropist and reformer, wrote a letter to Earl Grey about the horrors of the transportation system that had trafficked in convicts between Britain and Australia since the end of the eighteenth century. Recognizing the urgency of dispersing the nation's "redundant population," and conceding that the project of "peopling Australia with prisoners" had been one solution to the problem, Chisholm nonetheless called on the government to turn its attention to a more humane system of colonization. Her focus was on free emigration schemes, principally to help guarantee moral respectability in the colonies—an ambition threatened at every turn by the legacy of convict women.

> Think you, my Lord, that the most abandoned of the female race are fit companions for the children of [emigrant] men; a class of men who are, perhaps, more sensitively alive than any other to connecting their families in marriage to doubtful characters?... I repeat, what I have frequently stated, that to send abandoned women to the Colonies is an act of cruelty to them. Few indeed will be sought for as wives; respectable families will not receive them as servants.... Oh! It is frightful to look upon the monster evil which our penal policy has entailed upon that country ... it is full time that a subject of such high national and religious importance should occupy the attention of all well-thinking men, and that the regulations affecting emigrants should not be dictated by those who deem cheap labor as the chief consideration ....

Chisholm concluded her letter by calling for the imperial parliament to reform the emigration system lest it continue to resemble "a species of slavery." At the heart of her plea was a concern for the right and proper sexual order in the colonies to ward against the "demoralizing state of bachelorism" (Burton, 80).

As someone who had been involved with the challenges of emigration—she had started a Female Immigrant Home in Sydney in 1840—Chisholm knew how profoundly the history of convict women had shaped white settler society in the Antipodes. Between 1788 and 1868, 160,000 convicts were transported between British ports and Australian ones; 25,000 of those were women (Damousi). That gender asymmetry mirrored long histories of similar imbalances in slave colonies; in this context, it produced a "factory" system of semi-incarceration and surveillance that began on the ship and reached deep into the life and livelihoods of generations to come. Transportation was a form of colonization, driven at once by surplus population, and as Chisholm noted, by the need for cheap labor on the imperial periphery. The history of convict women tells the story how gendered the paradox of using unskilled workers in this service of colonial development was, and with what short- and long-term consequences (Oxley).

Convict passage was a form of forced migration designed to move the criminalized poor from both the urban centers and the hinterlands of the metropole to the outposts of empire in order to enhance the economic progress of both (see also **I is for Indenture**). Women may have been a minority of the convicts, but they embodied a variety of economic assets: They were young, literate, numerate, and often healthy. They frequently had had some occupational training as well. What caught them in the convict net was poverty. Rarely habitual criminals, nearly two-thirds were transported for a first offence, which was most often not violent: trivial crimes such as theft, pickpocketing, housebreaking or vagrancy. Among the goods stolen, the vast majority involved clothes or fabric such as blankets. The punishment was consistently disproportionate to the crime. Transportation meant banishment form home and family, from relations and familiars; the minimum sentence was seven years, while the maximum was fourteen. Nearly a third of convict women came from London, but many of those came from more rural locations, especially if they were Irish. Elizabeth Coltman received seven years for stealing silk; Caroline Humphries, fourteen for stealing gowns. The latter was her third offense. At just under five feet tall, she was a house girl who had not even stopped growing. And while she was undoubtedly desperate, like the convict women who joined her on the journey to New South

Wales or Van Diemen's Land, she would be considered a confirmed criminal, "depraved and disorderly" and destined for a life of hard labor, and possibly, more criminal indictments once landed. She would also be presumed to be a prostitute, whether she actually plied that trade or not (Damousi; Oxley). The ocean journey was a sign of things to come. By the time of Victoria's reign, incidence of onboard pregnancies had come to the attention of authorities to such a degree that the ship surgeon's manual expressly forbade prostitution and other forms of fraternizing, which could be punishable by flogging for the women. Under the gaze of these disciplinary regimes women, responded in ways that anticipated their protest at sea as factory women on land: They refused the food offered to them, stole bread, conspired to mutiny and otherwise disrupted the boundaries of body and space imposed on them. Once they disembarked, they were given clothes and taken to institutions such as Paramatta or Ross—compounds whose design echoed that of workhouses in the metropole and dedicated to the proposition that reform through female labor was the solution to the "problem" of convict women (Cassella). The "architecture of discipline" that the factories materialized was both radial and panoptical, modeling a penal philosophy in which surveillance was paramount; and individual liberty, contained and suppressed through a centralized authority. Containment was the key mechanism of factory control, the solitary cell the most paranoid form of its spatial discipline.

Convict women routinely disrupted this top-down fantasy of total oversight and subordination. They did so through jests and pranks— including the de-trousering of one Reverend William Bedford at the Cascades factory at Hobart in 1838 and "showing their naked posteriors" (mooning, by any other name). They swore and sang songs that ridiculed their jailers. When contracted out for service to local families, they stayed out all night, got drunk, dallied with men and even "whored," whether for pleasure or money. And when provoked, they might even murder, as Sarah McGregor did in 1834 when Charles Waldron threatened to report her to the police for bad behavior (Damousi). Like other economic rebels across the British Empire, convict women refused work, absconded and even fled as a way of withholding their labor from an exploitative system over which they had no structural control. Such small acts could be more or less effective in terms of women's actual freedom. Because of the paucity of convict testimony outside official records, we are left to interpret their acts as defiant evidence of their determination not to submit fully to the fate that the system of transportation Chisholm so abhorred had intended for them.

Suggestions for Further Reading

Chisholm, Caroline. *Emigration and Transportation*. London: John Ollivier, 1847.

Cassella, Elinor Conlin. "To Watch or Restrain: Female Convict Prisons in 19th Century Tasmania," *International Journal of Historical Archaeology* 5, 1 (2001): 45–72.

Damousi, Joy. *Depraved and Disorderly: Female Convicts, Sexuality and Gender in Colonial Australia*. Cambridge: Cambridge University Press, 1997.

Hughes, Robert. *The Fatal Shore: A History of the Transportation of Convicts to Australia, 1787–1868*. New York: Knopf, 1987.

McGrath, Ann, Marian Quartly, Marilyn Lake and Patricia Grimshaw. *Creating a Nation*. Victoria, Australia: McPhee Gribble, 1994.

Oxley, Deborah. *Convict Maids: The Forced Migration of Women to Australia*. Cambridge: Cambridge University Press, 1997.

C is also for . . .

Cannabis
"Cape to Cairo"
Cawnpore
Cetshwayo
"Clemency" Canning

D is for Dagga

This image of hemp with blue flowers looks innocent enough. Meanwhile, dagga smoking was prevalent across the empire and was subject to taxation by colonial regimes eager to control the kinds of social disorder it was thought to induce. Florilegius/SSPL/Getty Images.

Dagga—referred to alternately as cannabis, ganja, hemp and even "lion's tail," depending on the species—was commonly cultivated and widely used for various purposes throughout the British Empire. Shorthand most often for the narcotic drug, dagga was a source of endless fascination on the part of medical men, explorers and tourists who came across it in India and Africa. It was also a source of tremendous concern for colonial officials who sought to regulate its usage, especially among natives because, like alcohol and opium, it was considered an intoxicant whose effects threatened labor productivity, and in some places, normative public order as well. In fact, its physiological effects varied (and vary) from sleepiness to drunkenness to what one Dr. O'Shaughnessy, who tested dagga on dogs, servants, coolies and patients in 1840s India, called "harmless insensibility" (364). Dagga's medicinal powers were certainly recognized, but its capacity to undermine the rational social order, and as significantly, the work routines and regimens required by imperial capital, made it more than a mere object of curiosity. Dagga was considered a sign of native weakness, susceptibility to intoxication, and ultimately, unfitness for self-rule. The very commonness of its recreational and medicinal uses in indigenous communities meant that its policing was a preoccupation of those whose job it was to patrol the border between savage and civilized and guarantee that the labor required to maintain those distinctions proceeded unimpeded.

The origins of the word *dagga* are much debated. It may be derived from the southern African Khoi*daXa-b*, which is the root noun for *tobacco*, or it may stem from the Arabic *dukhkhan*. Certainly, it owes its wide circulation in Africa to the mobility of Arab traders who carried it along their networks and routes. Those early Europeans who heard the word among southern African peoples recorded it variously as *dacha*, *dakae*, *dagha* and *tacka*. On the East African coast, it was called *bange*, evocative of *bhang* used in parts of India. These terms, in turn, might refer to flowering tops or simply the leaves of a plant that they saw people smoking or chewing (Dutoit, 90 and ff.). Of course, dagga was traded as well as consumed, and hemp was a plant commonly used for textile production. But for imperial observers, how natives used dagga proved to be the greatest concern (see **O is for Opium**). In addition to remarking on the ordinary, even daily, consumption of dagga in native communities, observers also noted specific usages of particular interest in an imperial context, as when warriors sat down and smoked it before battle to improve their performance in the field.

Of equal concern was the danger to settlers and to Europeans more generally. David Livingstone produced this account of dagga (here, refereed to as *matokwane*) use among the Makololo near Victoria Falls in 1866:

> We had ample opportunity for observing the effects of this matokwane smoking on our men. It makes them feel very strong in body, but it produces exactly the opposite effect upon the mind ... the performances of a group of matokwane smokers are somewhat grotesque; they are provided with a calabash of pure water, a slot bamboo, five feet long, and the great pipe ... through which the smoke is drawn ... on its way to the mouth. Each smoker takes a few whiffs, the last being an extra long one, and hands the pipe to his neighbor. He seems to swallow the fumes; for, striving against the convulsive action of the muscles of chest and throat, he takes a mouthful of water from the calabash, waits a few seconds, and then pours water and smoke from his mouth down the groove of the bamboo. The smoke causes violent coughing in all, and in some a species of frenzy which passes away in a rapid stream, of unmeaning words, or short sentences, as

"the green grass grows," "the fat cattle thrive," "the fish swim." (Livingstone, 304)

Here, dagga is not just entertainment, but the basis of a parable about the perils of addiction. As Livingstone observes, as a result of their exposure to dagga, "two of our finest men became inveterate smokers, and partially idiotic."

The fact that dagga consumption was widespread, part of the regular everyday lives of many of the empire's indigenous subjects, was well known to colonial officials, who surveyed the districts they oversaw and catalogued its usage among any and all strata of local society. Colonial governments empire-wide were particularly keen to gather information about social, cultural and religious usage—not merely in order to create a catalog of colonial knowledge, but also because they understood that such practices traveled wherever colonial laborers did. The Indian Immigrants Commission in Natal, for example, did an extensive survey of hemp smoking out of concern that its impact on indentured Indian migrants was detrimental both to their capacity to work and to the general social order in the colony. The Commission took testimony from one resident magistrate about an Indian, "Bhalee by name," whose intoxication due to dagga caused him to assault a woman in the yard of a local estate—an assault that landed him in jail and prevented him from working for two weeks. If women smoked dagga, they were rarely recorded as doing so. Other aspects of white-settler colonial order were also threatened by the popularity of dagga. Africans traded with Indians for the drug, thus breaking down the racial boundaries between "subject" races and signaled an unofficial economy in which white traders were also involved, often at the greatest profit. Where the colonial state was deeply invested in establishing and maintaining racial distinction, dagga showed how precarious that segregationist policy could be on the ground.

What's more, dagga use offered colonial officials a window into what a global imperial challenge it actually was. Agents in Calcutta assessed the problem not just via the traffic in migrant labor from India to South Africa, but to and from the West Indies and Burma as well. They strove both to control the circulation of dagga, and of course, to profit from it via licensing fees and taxes. Nor was dagga's significance limited to the intracolonial mobility of labor: Once the British occupation of Egypt had been accomplished in 1882, officials there had to deal with the dagga (or hashish) market and the international net of smuggling of which it was a major node. At many scales of imperial power and hegemony, then, dagga was a threat to security, profit and business as usual. If the image above suggests a harmless plant, dagga's use was also a source of fascination and anxiety—as well as pleasure and escapism—for all manner of Victorians.

Suggestions for Further Reading

Dutoit, Brian M. "Dagga: Cannabis Sativa In Southern Africa," in Vera Rubin, ed., *Cannabis and Culture*. The Hague: Mouton Publications, 1975.

Goodman, Jordan, Paul E. Lovejoy and Andrew Sherratt, eds. *Consuming Habits: Global and Historical Perspectives on How Cultures Define Drugs*. London: Routledge, 1995.

Livingstone, David. *Narrative of an Expedition to the Zambesi and Its Tributaries*. New York: Harper and Brothers, 1866.

Mills, James. *Cannabis Britannica: Empire, Trade and Prohibition, 1800–1928*. Oxford: Oxford University Press, 2003.

Mills, James, and Patricia Barton, eds. *Drugs and Empires: Essays in Modern Imperialism and Intoxication*. London: Palgrave Macmillan, 2007.

O'Shaughnessy, W. B. "On the Preparations of the Indian Hemp, or Gunjah," *Provincial Medical Journal and Retrospect of the Medical Sciences* 123 (February 1843): 363–369.

Philip, John. *Researches in South Africa: Illustrating the Civil, Moral and Religious Condition of the Native Tribes*. London: James Duncan, 1828.

D is also for . . .

Davitt, Michael
Death of Gordon
Demerara
Dinshaway
Dock strikes
Dongola

E

is for Eyre—*Jane Eyre*

At the heart of the Charlotte Brontë novel Jane Eyre *is the Caribbean plantation complex, which helps to shape the course of Jane's love for Mr. Rochester, and in the end, her fate as one of the Victorian period's best-read heroines. Here, she is pictured with a rival suitor, St. John Rivers, whose missionary work in India tempts, but ultimately does not win, her. Illustration by Edmund Henry Garrett, January 1850, Hulton Archive.*

Charlotte Brontë published her first novel, *Jane Eyre*, under the pseudonym Currer Bell in October 1847, a mere six weeks after she submitted it: a phenomenally quick turnaround for a first-time author in any age, let alone the Victorian one. The book, for which her publisher Smith and Elder paid her £500, was an immediate sensation. It was regarded by the *Quarterly Review* as "preeminently an anti-Christian composition," no doubt because the heroine seeks her own fortune and rejects companionate marriage with the missionary St. John Rivers, choosing the more dubious character of Rochester instead. Despite, or perhaps because of, this daring plot line, Jane Eyre was a huge commercial success. It was in its third printing within six months, by which time the whole country was in the grip of "Jane Eyre fever" (Brennan, 96). William George Clark recorded his excitement for *Fraser's Magazine*: "We took up Jane Eyre one winter's evening, somewhat piqued by the extravagant commendations we had heard, and sternly resolved to be as critical as Croker. But as we read on we forgot both commendations and criticism, identifying ourselves with Jane and all her troubles, and finally married Mr. Rochester at about four in the morning" (Macdonald, 56).

Jane Eyre's biography is very much a class story: An orphan then a governess, Jane is on a path toward upward mobility, but she is also a status critic, embodying a kind of proletarian vision that nonetheless cherishes the bourgeois individualism at the heart of early Victorian respectability. Nineteenth-century gender ideologies are also on display in the novel: As a strong and determined female protagonist, Jane faces no greater challenge than to decide whether she wishes to marry, and if so, whom. For all the proto-feminism of the story, Jane's destination is conjugality and her path toward selfhood leads her to Rochester, albeit circuitously. But it's the fact of empire that structures Brontë's narrative, in ways that shape the class and gender story both. For Thornfield Hall is built on the profits derived from Rochester's

West Indian investments. It's home to Rochester's secret Creole wife, Bertha Mason, the "madwoman in the attic" whose history is hidden, but whose insanity brings the house down—literally, in flames, having been set on fire by Bertha, who then hurls herself off the roof, leaving Rochester free to marry Jane. Jane's developing sense of self is shaped by her encounters with Bertha, who tears at her wedding veil and appears as "savage" to Jane, undermining her faith in Rochester and bringing her face to face with the consequences of colonialism at home.

Bertha is a haunting figure; the "low, slow ha! Ha" with which she enters the text must have been part of the sensation that Victorian consumers experience as they devoured the book. Anticipating *Dracula* by half a century, Brontë has Jane comparing Bertha to a vampire, which places the novel squarely in the category of Victorian gothic. But it's as a specter of empire gone badly wrong that Bertha and the Caribbean interests she stands for undo the normative order of the English household. In that sense, *Jane Eyre* is a cautionary tale, reminding readers then and now that "it should not be possible to read nineteenth-century British literature without remembering that imperialism, understood as England's social mission, was a crucial part of the cultural representation of England to the English" (Azim; Spivak). It's also a reminder that colonial peoples traveled to and circulated through a variety of domestic English spaces in the Victorian period. Women and men native to India, African and the Caribbean—as well as people of color and of mixed parentage native to Britain—occupied the landscape of the mid-century United Kingdom, whether as travelers or temporary residents. Bertha Mason is not just a character who structures the narrative of Jane Eyre by accident. She is fictional evidence of the real, if often elusive, presence of colonial women who made the "imperial encounter" very real at home (Burton, 181).

In fact, the consequences of empire are to be found everywhere in *Jane Eyre*. Though slavery per se does not make an appearance, its role in the making of the modern subject is everywhere to be seen in the novel. The triumphant scene with Aunt Reed, her childhood tormentor, is evidence of how Jane's self-fashioning is articulated through languages of mastery and domination: "I felt a determination to subdue her—to be her mistress in spite of both her nature and her will." Not only is Jane's invocation of the master–slave relationship one of the conditions of Jane's subjectivity, Brontë Orientalizes it as well—with Rochester the tyrannical sultan, and Jane the resistant seraglio girl (Burton, 176). Not only that, Jane has her own fiscal ties to empire: It's her considerable inheritance from her uncle in Madeira that gives her the independence to make a truly "free" marriage choice.

Jane Eyre's imperial resonances go beyond the internal plotlines of the novel. Its readership circled the empire, drawing admirers and critics alike into a wider commons of print culture that followed the mobility of English subjects, especially to the white-settler colonies. We know from the correspondence of Brontë with her friend in New Zealand, the émigré Mary Taylor, that *Jane Eyre* and *Shirley*, "Currer Bell's" 1849 novel, were also sensations halfway around the world. They were advertised in Wellington's waterfront warehouses, avidly read and discussed, and their virtues and shortcomings just as passionately debated. For Mary, as perhaps for other women so far from home, Brontë's novels collapsed distances of time and space, linking the colonial and the provincial in uniquely intimate ways (Macdonald). Such intimacies continued in colonial spaces well into the twentieth century: *Jane Eyre* was a regular on reading lists in imperial curricula in Africa, and she makes a brief but telling appearance in Tsitsi Dangaremba's 1988 coming-of-age novel *Nervous Conditions* (Macdonald, 59). As well, Jean Rhys's *Wide Sargasso Sea*, published in 1966, turns *Jane Eyre* on its head by centering the story on Bertha Mason in Jamaica and the Windward Islands. Here named Antoinette Cosway, she backlights her Creole origins and the historical conditions that gave rise to her fictional fate at Thornfield Hall. In a direct aim at the logo-centricity of Victorian imperial culture, books in this context are not only unread, they are tossed aside, to be eaten by insects. What would Jane Eyre make of that?

Suggestions for Further Reading

Azim, Firdous. *The Colonial Rise of the Novel.* London: Routledge, 1993.

Brennan, Zoe. *Brontë's Jane Eyre.* London: Bloomsbury, 2010.

Gilbert, Sandra, and Susan Gubar. *The Madwoman in the Attic: The Woman Writer and the 19th century Literary Imagination.* New Haven: Yale, 1984.

Macdonald, Charlotte. "*Jane Eyre* at Home and Abroad" in Antoinette Burton and Isabel Hofmeyr, eds, *Ten Books that Shaped the British Empire.* Durham: Duke University Press, 2014.

Said, Edward. *Culture and Imperialism.* New York: Vintage Books, 1994.

Spivak, Gayatri. "Three Women's Texts and a Critique of Imperialism," *Critical Inquiry* 12, 1 (1985): 243–261.

E is also for . . .

East India Company
The Eastern Question
Egyptian occupation
Eviction
Eyre, Edward

F is for Famine

At its height, The Illustrated London News *had more than 200,000 weekly readers in Britain and beyond. Here, those readers could see in vivid detail people seeking relief from famine in Bengal in 1874 by praying to a stone statue of a bull outside a temple dedicated to Shiva. From* The Illustrated London News, *London, February 21, 1874.*

By a lonely prison wall
I heard a young maid calling,
"Michael they are taking you way,
For your stole Trevelyan's corn
That the young might see the morn.
Now the prison ship lies waiting in the bay."

Though often attributed to natural disaster or the exigencies of environmental change, famine is rarely simply inevitable. When understood in the context of the history of the Victorian empire, famine is state failure by any other name. The most recognizable images of nineteenth-century famine are undoubtedly from Ireland, where *An Gorta Mór*, or the Great Hunger, produced death, disease and immigration on a huge scale, and in ways that would reverberate in Britain and beyond for decades to come.

The result of the invasion of the fungal spore *phytophthora infestans,* the potato famine impacted successive harvests between 1845 and 1850, and drove a quarter of the Irish population to death or to escape by boat to the United States, England or Australia. The potato itself was a symptom of colonial rule: Since the eighteenth century, it had been fundamental to the diet of mainly Catholic Irish peasants in thrall to the system of Protestant landlordism. It was the fuel of a cheap labor force that served a settler agrarian economy and tied it, perilously, to a single form of sustenance on which almost two million people depended for their daily survival. Potato dependency was, in short, emblematic of a wider developmental economics designed to keep the cost of foodstuffs low for the English consumer at the expense of Irish livelihoods, and in the wake of the famine, of Irish lives as well.

British response to the potato blight was alternately censorious and pragmatic. Charles Trevelyan, assistant secretary to the Treasury and famine relief administrator, shared the prejudices of many Victorians in his view that Irish Catholics were a lazy race of people whose calamity was an act of God. "It is hard upon the poor people," he wrote, "that they should be deprived of knowing that they are suffering from an affliction of God's Providence." Under his direction, government assistance was run along laissez-faire principles, with economy and discipline rather than "relief" at its core. Where public works were required, they might require backbreaking work for wages or the withholding of pay for paltry food. Prime Minister Robert Peel, for his part, appreciated economics of the situation. His quest for the repeal of the Corn Laws (and hence, of duties on corn) as well as the £100,000 he expended to send Indian maize to supplement Irish diets went some way toward alleviation, though the Irish called it "Peel's brimstone" because of its painful gastric effects. Lord Monteagle moved those who could travel off his land with promises of a deposit on the cost of passage to Australia, though many like Michael in the lyric above, ended up with transportation for life when they were found poaching game or fish on landlords' estates to survive. Meanwhile, Trevelyan was knighted for his service to the nation.

The London Illustrated News captured the stories and images of the famine years with the due diligence that the government lacked. It sent reporters and sketch artists across the land and delivered harrowing tales of emaciation and despair to middle-class consumers of political and economic news throughout the Hungry Forties. Irish leaders such as Daniel O'Connell raised protests in Dublin and London about the "death-dealing famine" as typhus wracked the land and evictions on the grounds of disease proceeded apace, reaching 3,500 by 1846. Those who were not enfeebled by starvation or dysentery often took the law into their own hands. Major Denis Mahon, who was an aggressive evictor in County Roscommon, was ambushed and killed by local residents, as was Reverend John Lloyd, whom many felt was using local soup kitchen provisions as a factory for converting vulnerable Catholics to Protestantism.

If the Great Famine became a watchword for imperial racism and state failure for Irish nationalists and others seeking permanent relief from imperial rule, the Irish Hunger is only the most commonly known food crisis in the context of British colonial hegemony. Bengal under East India Company rule had been the site of a devastating famine in 1770. Brought on in part by crop failure and rain, it was exacerbated by rampant taxation, which strained food surpluses. These conditions eventually drove struggling peasants off their land and the Indian rural economy into a death spiral. Such conditions were also ripe for unrest, as evidenced by the Sannyasi rebellion chronicled in fictional form in Bankim Chandra Chatterjee's novel *Andamanath* a century later (see **V is for "Vande Mataram"**). Nor was this kind of structurally produced colonial hunger epiphenomenal. Victorian Bengal witnessed serial famines between the 1860s and 1890s. *The Graphic*, a London-based photojournalism organ, covered the devastation of 1877 with particular vividness, offering readers dramatic photographs of malnourished children whose power arguably rivaled the *Illustrated London News* sketches of Ireland because they archived the living as they were dying. The Famine Commission of 1901, in its phlegmatic overview of nineteenth-century food crises, openly admitted that government relief was "insufficient" and "imperfectly organized," blaming "the inability of private trade, hampered by want of railways and transportation, to supply the demand for food" (2). Accountability was laid at the feet of Indian society, which, "resting as it does upon the moral of mutual assistance, is admirably adapted for common effort against a common misfortune." In the absence of colonial adaptation, the commissioners echoed Trevelyan's laissez-faire commitments when they warned against any measure that might "check the growth of thrift and self-reliance among the people."

If the commissioners seemed resigned to the recurrent failure of the state to meet the challenges and anticipate the next famine on the horizon, it was in part because they attributed famine's inevitability to the ecological conditions to which India was subject—whether monsoon or drought. Their response was practical—develop better systems of intelligence, more effective relief works, better reserves of "tool and plant"—rather than preventive. As in the struggle for the Northwest Frontier (see **A is for the Afghan Wars** and **Y is for Yakub Kahn**), those responsible for the conquest, maintenance and productivity of the Victorian empire blamed environmental forces beyond their control, even as they continued to profit when and where they could from the raw materials of the soil they occupied as alien invaders.

Suggestions for Further Reading

Keneally, Thomas. *Three Famines: Starvation and Politics.* New York: PublicAffairs, 2011.

Klein, Ira. "Plague, Policy and Popular Unrest in British India," *Modern Asian Studies* (1988) 22, 4: 723–755.

Nally, David P. *Human Encumbrances: Political Violence and the Great Irish Famine.* South Bend: Notre Dame, 2011.

Report of the Indian Famine Commission. Calcutta, 1901.

Vernon, James. *Hunger: A Modern History.* Cambridge, MA: Belknap, 2007.

F is also for . . .

Fashoda
First Opium War
The Four Feathers
Free Trade
Fugitive Offenders Act

G is for Gandhi

Gandhi made part of his Victorian career as a barrister and early nationalist in South Africa. There, he discovered the racism of the British Empire in ways that had not been evident to him in either India or London, where he had trained at the Inns of Court. This photo, taken in 1908, followed on a beating he received when he went to register as an Indian under the "Black Act" in the Transvaal. Photo by Dinodia Photos.

Gandhi is not necessarily thought of as a Victorian, but he definitely was one. Of course, he was technically a subject of her Majesty the Queen. But his life and his politics—which most associate with the twentieth-century movement for Indian independence—were, significantly, a product of Victorian culture and imperialism. His experiences in Britain and South Africa in the 1880s and 1890s were to transform him into an advocate for self-government. That vocation, together with his advocacy of nonviolence as an anticolonial strategy, would make him one of the best-known figures in the British Empire, propelling him onto the world stage and linking his name to the postcolonial Indian project for decades beyond his death.

He was born Mohandas Karamchand Gandhi in Gujarat in 1869 to a merchant family, his father was a diwan, a ministerial position in the British Princely state of Porbander. His mother was an extremely devout Hindu; her religious sensibilities and practices doubtless had an enormous impact on Gandhi's development as a spiritual person and political leader. According to his sister, the young Gandhi was like "restless mercury." After an undistinguished career at school and college, his family decided the best way for him to prepare for a diwanship of his own was to train as a barrister in London. By this time, Gandhi had entered into a child marriage; his wife, Kasturba, and he were married as teens and they had four surviving children, the eldest of whom was born just as he was leaving for England.

Travel to Britain represented a spiritual challenge to practicing Hindus because it involved crossing the *kala pani*—the "black waters"—which were thought of as pollutants, and hence, a threat to caste status. In fact, some family elders effectively forbad him to depart, and when he declined to follow their wishes, he was declared an outcast. While in London, Gandhi struggled to keep the promises he had made to his mother to practice sexual abstinence as well as to refrain from consuming meat or alcohol—all expressions of Hindu devotion that she prized. Gandhi's autobiography, *My Experiments with Truth*, records his encounters with metropolitan social life, in drawing rooms and on the streets of the capital city. As vigilant as he may have been about his pledges to his mother, the question of dress was equally preoccupying: He bought a suit in Bond Street and set about learning how to become an English gentleman (94)—including taking dancing and elocution lessons. Given his later embrace of ascetic dress in the name of swadeshi, Gandhi was surely being mischievous when he wrote that this "punctiliousness in dress lasted for years."

His time in London as a student was consequential to the nationalist he was to become in other ways. He attended meetings of the National Indian Association—a social milieu where Indian students mingled with English social reformers and some Indian political figures such as Dadhabai Naoroji, one of the early presidents of the Indian National Congress. But Gandhi's political education took different forms as well. He was impressed by what he called the "simple living" of his fellow students: modest conditions that he strove to imitate by surviving on a meager shilling a day—an asceticism that brought him pleasure, helped keep the distractions of London life at bay and laid the groundwork for his later political philosophy. He joined a vegetarian society and began to think deeply about the relationship between diet and ethics. He was also "moved to lust" by some of the English women he met, temptations that threw him further into asceticism and into reflections on all the world's religions, including Christianity. He was drawn to New Testament doctrines emphasizing humility and the power of the "poor in spirit." England was also the place where, ironically, he read and studied the *Bhagavad Gita* for the first time.

Gandhi passed the bar exam in 1891 and sailed immediately for home. But his mother's death (which occurred before his return but was kept from him) was devastating. His attempts at practicing law in Bombay were unsuccessful. He answered an ad for a post at an Indian law firm in Natal, South Africa. He remained there for more than twenty years, from 1893 to 1914, and it was here, in this outpost of the late Victorian empire, that his future as a nationalist was made.

Natal in the 1890s was a racially mixed white-settler colony where tensions between Indian communities and the British establishment were beginning to run high. The firm he worked for, the Pretoria-based Dada Abdulla and Co., was run by wealthy Muslim merchants seeking to protect their economic interests in an atmosphere structured by hierarchies of race, class and caste—with indentured Indian workers a demographic majority with few legal let alone political rights (see **I is for Indenture**). Though by all accounts he had not faced outright racial discrimination in Britain, Gandhi experienced it firsthand soon after his arrival in South Africa when he tried to board a train to Pretoria with a first-class ticket. He was summarily thrown off the train onto the station platform at Maritzburg because a white passenger objected to a "coloured" man traveling in the whites-only compartment.

Much has been made of Gandhi's awakening to the racism at the heart of colonial settler rule in the wake of this incident. Certainly, it was important to his political education and even to his later commitments to nonviolence. But in the end, Gandhi was complexly Victorian. Throughout the rest of the 1890s, he led the fight for rights for Indians in Natal, but this did not entail a critique of imperialism per se. He joined an ambulance corps during the Boer War and recruited Indians in support of his efforts; he also supported Indian recruitment in 1906 during the Bambatha rebellion, a Zulu-led uprising against the British in Natal. And while he condemned British racism against Indians, he shared many Victorians' views of Africans as degraded and inferior; he strove to ensure that Indians were not treated with the same contempt and violence as "the raw kaffir[s]" precisely because he did not wish Indians to be seen as their equivalents. Empire was consequential to the birth of Indian nationalism. In Gandhi's case, his imperial affinities were as powerful as his forms of dissent and disruption, and they informed both.

Suggestions for Further Reading

Bhana, Surendra, and Goolam Vahed. *The Making of a Political Reformer: Gandhi in South Africa, 1893–1914*. Delhi: Manohar, 2005.

Desai, Ashwini, and Goolam Vahed. *The South African Gandhi: Stretcher-Bearer of Empire*. Palo Alto: Stanford, 2015.

Guha, Ramachandra. *Gandhi Before India*. New York: Knopf, 2014.

Hunt, James. *Gandhi in London*. New Delhi: Promilla, 1978.

Izkin, Erik. *Gandhi's Johannesburg: Birthplace of Satyagraha*. Johannesburg: Witwatersrand University Press, 2000.

G is also for . . .

Gatling gun
Ghazni
Goldstein, Vida
Gordon, George William
The Great Game
Gurkha

H is for Hosay

COOLIE HOSEIN FESTIVAL, TRINIDAD, B. W. I.

These tombs—also known as tazias or tadjahs—were photographed on the occasion of Hosay in Trinidad in 1912. The popular festival was a creolized version of commemorations of the death of one of Mohammed's grandsons in India and the Middle East. A free-spirited and often riotous celebration, it was the occasion for imperial crackdowns and massacre in the 1880s. The Alma Jordan Library, the University of the West Indies, St Augustine.

San Fernando is Trinidad's second city and was the center of the island's chief sugar-growing district, where, by the early 1880s, most of its Indian (South Asian) indentured and free laborers were concentrated. October 30, 1884, was the day on which the climax of the annual Muharram festival, known as Hosay in Trinidad, would take place: several grand processions of thousands of men carrying ornate, carefully made tombs (*tazias* or, in Trinidad, *tadjahs*) through the streets of the city toward the shoreline, where they would be dumped into the sea. There would be *tassa* drumming, mock stick fighting, singing, yelling, for the Hosay was "passion play, festival and street theatre rolled into one" (Singh, 26). Though it was in origin a Muslim Shi'ite festival mourning the death of the Prophet's grandson Husayn at Karbala in modern Iraq, in Trinidad, most people taking part were Hindus; many African-Trinidadians joined in too, and San Fernando's multiracial population enjoyed watching the action from the safety of street balconies and windows.

But this Hosay was different. Regulations had been issued in July 1884 that prohibited the processions from entering San Fernando, the accustomed route for many years. The authorities were determined to enforce these novel restrictions; detachments of armed police and British soldiers and marines had been stationed at the main entrances to the city the previous day, and on the morning of October 30, they were ready, along with magistrates to read the Riot Act. For their part, though some of the participants had heard vaguely of the new rules, none seriously believed that the police would "shoot people like fowls" (quoted Singh, 18). They were wrong.

As the processions approached the Cipero Street and Mon Repos entrances to San Fernando, what with the customary drumming, stick fighting, chanting and yelling, it's unlikely anyone heard the two magistrates stationed at each place reading the Act—ending in the usual request for God to save the Queen—let alone understood it (few Indian immigrants understood much English in this period). At both places the police fired into the front ranks of the still moving processions. Men and tadjahs fell together; "bloodstained tombs" mingled with the dead and the injured (Singh, 17–22, 87–135). At least 16 men were killed and about 100 were injured, making this massacre the most serious collision in terms of casualties in Trinidad's long and far from peaceful colonial history.

Indentured Indian immigration to Trinidad began in 1845, just seven years after the final end of slavery (see **I is for Indenture**). By 1880, the indentureds and their locally-born children constituted well over a quarter of the island's population, with the proportion being much higher in the sugar districts around San Fernando. The great majority still lived on the sugar plantations, including ex-indentured laborers who had opted not to return to India, and locally-born Indians.

Muslims were a small minority among the immigrants, and most of them were Sunni rather than Shi'ite. But Hosay (Muharram), a long-established and important festival in northern India, was brought to Trinidad very early, within a year or two of 1845. By 1880, it had developed into a significant, pan-Indian annual fête, with enthusiastic participation by the majority Hindus; some working-class Creoles (those of African and mixed African/European descent) joined in, especially involved in the drumming and stick fighting that resonated with their own cultural practices. Hosay was celebrated all over Trinidad where there were sugar plantations and Indian residents, but the San Fernando processions were the biggest. Gangs from different plantations engaged in rivalry with each other in the building of the tadjahs, the elaborate dances and the ritual stick fighting. Although brawls did occasionally break out, the colonial newspapers reveal no special anxiety about the Hosay up to the late 1870s.

But the early 1880s saw a depression in the West Indian sugar industry due to lower prices caused by competition from European beet imports. The brunt was born by the laborers, by then mostly Indian in Trinidad, who faced reduced earnings and increased tasks. A wave of protests—strikes, attacks on plantation personnel, absenteeism—created considerable anxiety among the planters and the authorities by 1884. Indeed, the island newspapers during that year published many pieces reflecting a kind of hysteria about the dangers of a newly militant and assertive Indian labor force—the same men earlier judged "docile" and tractable (Singh, 9–14, 54–69).

This was the context for the decision to place new restrictions on the Hosay processions, and to prepare for confrontation and even bloodshed if the marchers defied the rules and tried to enter San Fernando in 1884. In addition, between 1881 and 1884, the authorities had carried out a crackdown on aspects of the annual Carnival, the cherished festival of the Creole masses; the "Indian Carnival" should also be controlled and restricted, especially at a time when planters and officials were nervous about the volatility of the Indian laborers. And the enthusiastic participation of "Creole roughs" in Hosay, the prospect of Indian/African rapprochement even if only once a year, made the authorities even more fearful.

The aftermath of the massacre was depressingly familiar. Most of the island press fully supported the police actions and felt the bloodshed had been necessary to curb the menace of Indian aggression. But a letter by a Trinidadian who had worked in India, denouncing the killing of unarmed men engaged in a customary festival, was published in the UK *Times*, forcing London to agree to an enquiry. The governor of Jamaica (an old "India hand") conducted a perfunctory investigation that fully exonerated the actions of the colonial government and the police (Singh, 136–149).

What happened on October 30, 1884, was largely forgotten for decades after. Hosay gradually died out in most places, including San Fernando, and is now only celebrated in a suburb of the capital, Port of Spain (Korom, 128–245). In the colonial historiography, and indeed long after national independence (1962), the event was recalled, if at all, as the "Hosay Riots." But more recently, the much more accurate

"Hosay Massacre" is the preferred term, and the "bloodstained tombs" have come to be seen as a symbol of colonial brutality and Indo-Trinidadian resistance. Annual marches on October 30, to the two sites of memory in San Fernando where the massacres took place, have been held to commemorate the victims/martyrs in recent years.

Suggestions for Further Reading

De Verteuil, Anthony. *Eight East Indian Immigrants*. Trinidad and Tobago: Paria Publishing, 1989.

Kale, Madhavi. *Fragments of Empire*. Philadelphia: University of Pennsylvania Press, 1994.

Korom, Frank. *Hosay Trinidad Muharram Performances in an Indo-Caribbean Diaspora*. Philadelphia: University of Pennsylvania Press, 2002.

Singh, Kelvin. *Bloodstained Tombs: The Muharram Massacre 1884*. London: Macmillan Caribbean, 1988.

Tikasingh, Gerad. *Trinidad During the 19th Century The Indian Experience*. La Romaine, Trinidad (The author) 2012.

H is also for . . .

Haowhenua
Havelock, Henry
Herat
Hintsa
Home Rule

I is for Indenture

Indenture was a brutal labor regime that took many forms across the British Empire in the nineteenth century. This picture, taken in South Africa in the 1890s as part of a lantern slide show series, is staged to underscore a familial scene that masks the terrible conditions under which most "coolies" labored.

The history of indenture in the British Empire is deeply entangled in other forms of forced labor, including slavery and convict labor, and the contingent racialized regimes that emerged from colonial management of those labor forces (see **Q is for Queensland Sugar and C is for Convict Women**). Indentured laborers signed contracts to work without pay for a period of years, often but not always in exchange for room, board or paid migration. Indenture, like other forms of forced labor, was constitutive of global capitalism and colonial racial hierarchies. At the same time, indentured laborers developed multiple strategies of resistance and refusal, while the figure of indentured labor repeatedly unsettled imperial categories of white/black, free/slave and colony/metropole.

The process of indenture was one of uprooting and transplanting, inherently disruptive and potentially transgressive of racial and national boundaries. Indentured emigrants from Britain were a crucial part of early white settlement in the Americas. They were contracted for four to seven years' work primarily on sugar, cotton and tobacco plantations in the Chesapeake Bay and the West Indies. As the eighteenth century progressed, colonial master and servant laws increasingly differentiated between indentured and slave labor, creating a legal system that enshrined a black-white dichotomy (Brown). With the increase in black chattel slavery, the spectacle of bonded white labor had become an embarrassing threat to white settler colonialism.[1] By the early nineteenth century, as the abolition movement gained momentum, planters and politicians alike looked for alternative sources of labor. In the 1830s, British officials began to

---

[1] Other forms of white bonded labor, such as convict labor or impressed sailors and soldiers, continued well into the nineteenth century. However, in these forms as well, distinctions were increasingly made between the treatment of white and nonwhite bonded labor (Anderson, 93–109).

discuss the importation of indentured laborers from India and China to the West Indies and various Indian Ocean islands. Like black slaves, Indian and Chinese indentured laborers could be marked as racially "Other," while unlike slaves, these laborers were ostensibly "free." By the 1840s, Indian and Chinese indentured labor was being sent to the British and French West Indies, Mauritius, South America, Australia, South Africa and East Africa as well as to locations within India and Southeast Asia (see **G is for Gandhi**).

Emigration was highest from impoverished districts or in times of famine. Recruiters targeted those who were in trouble with their family, landlords or the government, with high numbers of Chinese indenturing in the wake of the Taiping Rebellion. There were frequent complaints of abuses by recruiters, including deception, forged signatures and passengers dosed with opium. However, this narrative of victimhood ignores the role of returning migrants in enlisting indentured laborers in order to maintain family structures (Carter). Once onboard the ship, passengers faced confinement, bad and often religiously unclean food, and the unknown distance to their destination. For observant Hindus, the crossing of the *kala pani*, or "black water," meant losing caste, although as overseas travel became more prevalent, emigrants developed rituals for re-instating caste. Contracts lasted up to eight years and some colonies, like South Africa, had laws to pressure immigrants to re-indenture. Plantation labor remained the most prevalent, but laborers also worked in mines, on railroads or for government agencies. Workers were bound to the employer and the place they worked, requiring passes from their employers to travel off the plantation. Punishments were harsh, and physical abuse was frequent. The Chinese government banned contract emigration to the Americas in 1873, but indenture still continued elsewhere into the twentieth century. Nationalist agitation succeeded in pressuring the Indian government to ban indentured emigration by 1917, and indenture within India formally ended in 1920.

Following the lead of twentieth-century reformers, historians have continued to debate whether indenture was a "new system of slavery" (Tinker). Nineteenth-century advocates of indenture were careful to emphasize the contractual aspect of indenture, while Indian nationalists and British philanthropists decried indenture as slavery by any other name. Madhavi Kale argues that the debate over whether indenture is slavery or not is itself a product of the historical construction of "free" labor that British imperialists developed through the abolition of slavery. This bifurcated model of free versus slave labor fails to allow for a continuum of coercion. According to Kale, the contract became a shibboleth of free labor, allowing for all kinds of abuses as long as a "voluntarily" signed contract proved the willingness of the laborer (Kale). However, while the liberal imperial state interpreted the indenture contract as evidence of the triumph of free labor, the contract, or *girmit*, was for indentured Indians a symbol of a space and time apart, often likened to *narak*, or hell (Mishra). Indentured Indians referred to themselves as *girmitiya*, or "contracted." For those experiencing indenture, the contract was not an external, alienable condition of employment; it was an experiential identity that located one in an alternate dimension of suffering.

Indentured laborers were quick to develop forms of adaptation and resistance, disrupting the racialized labor regimes that imperial power attempted to impose. Indirect forms of resistance included breaking tools, working slowly, desertion and sickness. Holiday celebrations were both a source of syncretic cultural celebration and a refusal to conform to the oppressive regime of continual productivity. The festival of Mohurrum, for example, became an occasion of loud celebration for Hindus and Afro-Caribbeans as well as Muslim indentured laborers (see **H is for Hosay**). Early twentieth-century accounts of indenture such as Benarsi Das Chaturvedi's biography of a Fiji indentured laborer or Bechu's letters to the *Daily Chronicle* on contract violations raised nationalist awareness among elites as well as subaltern populations. This activism was instrumental in getting indenture abolished. Faced with the violent dispersal of indenture, diasporic subjects nonetheless built transnational networks that challenged imperial hegemony.

Resistance could also turn violent. In 1913, when Mohandas Gandhi invited South African indentured workers to join his passive resistance movement, the uprising quickly expanded beyond Gandhi's goals or methods (Swan). Violence, however, was more often internally directed. Fights were common, with communal and shipboard rivalries carried to new locations and exacerbated by the economic and social disjunctures of indenture. Instances of rape, sexual assault and domestic violence were also frequent. Suicide rates among indentured laborers were 2 to 20 percent higher than among Indians in the subcontinent. It can be difficult to categorize these violent acts, born of desperation, prejudice or misogyny, as resistance. However, such instances of violence did disrupt plantation discipline and deprive owners, temporarily or permanently, of the labor they desired to control. Not all resistance is triumphal.

Other forms of resistance and adaptation created flourishing Indian and Chinese communities, many of which became permanent settlements after the period of indenture was over. These workers cherished cultural practices from their homeland, while also creating new syncretic cultures. The centrality of the corneta china in Cuban conga performances, the Durban dish called "bunny chow" that consists of curry in a half-loaf of bread and the rhythms of Trinidadian chutney music: all are cultural practices that continue today. They are legacies of resilience and renewal in the face of the horrors of forced labor. Indenture was a system of violent expropriation and alienation of labor, and yet, those under indenture developed expressions of resistance, refusal and regeneration that challenged and transcended empire.

Suggestions for Further Reading

Anderson, Clare. "Convicts and Coolies: Rethinking Indentured Labour in the Nineteenth Century," *Slavery and Abolition* 30, 1 (2009): 93–109.

Bahadur, Gaiutra. *Coolie Woman: The Odyssey of Indenture*. Chicago: University of Chicago Press, 2013.

Carter, Marina. *Voices from Indenture: Experiences of Indian Migrants in the British Empire*. Leceister: Leicester University Press, 1996.

Kale, Madhavi. *Fragments of Empire: Capital, Slavery, and Indian Indentured Labor in the British Caribbean*. Philadelphia: University of Pennsylvania Press, 1998.

Mishra, Sudesh. "Time and Girmit," *Social Text 82* 23, 1 (Spring 2005): 15–36.

Swan, Maureen. "The 1913 Natal Indian Strike," *Journal of Southern African Studies* 10, 2 (April 1984): 239–258.

Tinker, Hugh. *A New System of Slavery: The Export of Indian Labour Overseas, 1830–1920*. Oxford: Oxford University Press, 1974.

Yun, Lisa. *The Coolie Speaks: Chinese Indentured Laborers and African Slaves in Cuba*. Philadelphia: Temple University Press, 2009.

I is also for . . .

Indigo
Indirect Rule
Inayat Kila
Irish Land League
Isandlwana

J is for Jihad

SOULÈVEMENTS DANS L'INDE ANGLAISE
Prédication de la guerre sainte

The call to jihad was common across the Northwest Frontier in the last decades of Victoria's reign, prompted in part by the British determination to control, if not to conquer or settle, Afghanistan. This preacher caught the attention of Le Petit Journal, *a major French daily newspaper with hundreds of thousands of readers. It reminds us of the ways that jihad has always been a concern for those with an eye on the international political order. Artist F. Meaulle,* Le Petit Journal, *October 3, 1897. Print Collector.*

The call to jihad was one feature of Muslim response to British territorial expansion projects in the Victorian period. Facing the prospect of the British occupation of Egypt in 1882, for example, Colonel Ahmed Urabi (see **U is for Urabi**) wrote to William Gladstone, then Prime Minister, via a letter to *The Times*, warning that as allowed by the Koran, Egyptians would take up a holy war if the issues around debt and parliamentary forms of government could not be peaceably resolved. Those who followed the crisis in the Sudan which ensued, in which the Mahdi (in Arabic, the guided one, who will rule before the end of the world), Muhammad Ahmad bin Abd Allah, preached spiritual renewal and ultimately waged war against the British and their allies. The Mahdist war—labeled by one historian as "Victorian jihad"—preoccupied Britons at home in part because it involved a national hero-martyr, Major-General Charles George Gordon. Gordon had gained fame through his contributions to the suppression of the Taiping Rebellion. When revolt broke out in the Sudan, Gordon was dispatched to help evacuate civilians and soldiers. A siege ensued, which lasted a year, and Gordon was killed. Not only that, he was beheaded and his body was thrown down a well. Such was the spectacular end to this particular instance of British resistance to jihad.

Gordon was memorialized across the British Isles and across the empire, which means that the effects of jihad left monumental, if indirect, traces in the landscapes and social geographies of Victorians well after the details of his martyrdom were forgotten. The 1887 statute in Melbourne received so many public subscriptions that the sculptor was able to add four panels tracing various stages of his career as a soldier for empire. But most Victorians would like to associate jihad as much with India and the Northwest Frontier as they would with the Sudan. Fears of jihad were rampant in 1857, when mutineers who were both Hindu and Muslim drew on a variety of repertoires of struggle and resistance, holy war included. Because of their supposed fidelity to the Ottoman caliphate, Muslim loyalty to the Raj was often in question. In fact, it gave rise to an extensive debate in the early 1870s as to whether Muslims were "bound by their religion to rebel against the Queen." Sir W. W. Hunter wrote a short book entitled *The Indian Mussulmans* in which he portrayed India north and east of Calcutta to be practically swarming with jihadis in an intermittent but sustained warfare against the infidel invaders. In Hunter's view, British hegemony was ever precarious; Muslims were a "source of chronic danger": And even a minor infraction might "free them from their duty as subjects, and bind them over to treason and Holy War."

Key to this history was Syed Ahmad Barelvi, whose main enemy was in fact the Sikhs who, under the leadership of Ranjit Singh, consolidated their kingdom at the expense of traditionally Muslim lands contingent with Afghanistan (see **A is for the Afghan Wars**). Though he was eventually killed by the Sikh army, Barelvi was strategic and cosmopolitan in his approach to jihad: He cultivated a multitude of local and regional supporters and waged war against successive occupiers (i.e., the Sikhs and then the British; Devji, 36–37). Hunter's little book, which featured Barelvi prominently, provoked a public response from Sayyid Ahmed Khan, who denied claims that Muslims were, qua Muslims, inclined to jihad, though he did suggest that when holy war arose it stemmed from British ignorance of Muslim communities and a "want of sympathy and union between rulers and ruled" (Devji). As well, he directly contradicted Hunter on the career of Barelvi whose anti-British sentiments he played down, arguing that his holy war was limited to the Sikhs and that it was his successors who mainly stirred up jihadi sentiments. An educated nobleman who had entered the English civil service and was a member of the Viceroy's Legislative Council, Sayyid Ahmad had also written a book on the causes of the 1857 mutiny in order to dispel arguments that it was the product of a Muslim conspiracy. Despite his reputation as a modernizer, his pro-British attitudes were not widely shared among Muslims, especially those who took a pan-Islamic view of Muslim community as opposed to an Indian-centered one. Victorian debates over jihad, and over the right and proper posture toward British rule more generally, divided Muslims and helped to shape the contours of Indian nationalism in the twentieth century in the process.

In contrast, the question of jihad was hardly academic on the Northwest Frontier in the nineteenth century. Dost Mohammed, Britain's erstwhile ally and then enemy in the first Afghan war, declared jihad shortly after the British installed their puppet king, Shah Shuja, in Kabul in 1839. Whispers of holy war animated many of the intermittent struggles between the two wars as well as in the campaigns themselves. In the face of British invasion in 1878, Sher Ali—son of Dost Mohammed and the emir of Afghanistan—called on his followers to "Wage a holy war on behalf of God and his prophet, with your property and your lives.... Let the rich equip the poor. Let all die for the holy cause. A foreign nation, without cause or the slightest provocation, has made up its mind to invade our country and conquer it" (Burton; see also **Y is for Yakub Khan**). The British feared fanaticism in every inch of the frontier. They found their fears justified in the figure of the "mad mullah," also known as the "fakir of Swat," a messianic itinerant who galvanized thousands of tribesmen with his anti-British rhetoric in the late 1890s. His image made its way into metropolitan print culture when *The Graphic* depicted him proselytizing and bands of Afghanis clamoring for his attention and, presumably, war. Though it was not universally a response to European imperialism, here, jihad was a challenge to British aggression, specifically the establishment of the Durand Line (1893), which effectively partitioned Afghanistan into separate British and emir-controlled spheres. The call for holy war was not, then, unprovoked. Rooted in currents of Islamic revivalism, it was one direct response to the Great Game and British territorial ambition more generally among Muslim religious and political leaders and their adherents in parts of the Victorian empire.

Selections for Further Reading

Alavi, Seema. *Muslim Cosmopolitanism in an Age of Empire*. Cambridge: Harvard University Press, 2015.

Burton, Antoinette, ed. *The First Anglo-Afghan Wars*. Durham: Duke University Press, 2014.

Devji, Faisal. *Landscapes of the Jihad: Militancy, Morality, Modernity*. Ithaca: Cornell, 2005.

Edwards, David B. *Heroes of the Age: Moral Faultlines on the Afghan Frontier*. Berkeley: University of California Press, 1996.

Hunter, W. W. *The Indian Musulmans*. London: Trubner, 1876.

Jalal, Ayesha. *Partisans of Allah: Jihad in South Asia*. Cambridge: Harvard University Press, 2010.

J is also for . . .

Jamaica
Jameson Raid
Jellalabad
Jhansi, Rani of
Jingoism

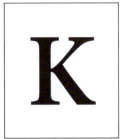

K is for Kīngitanga

Tawhiao I (1822–1894) the Maori king of New Zealand, leader of the Wiakato tribes. Tawhiao has the fine facial tattooing of the high-ranking Maori.

Kīngitanga, or the King Movement, emerged in the 1850s as a concerted effort to build political unity among Māori iwi in the face of British colonialism. Prior to sustained contact with Europeans from 1769, Māori social and political life was ordered around whānau (family), hapū (subtribe, clan) and iwi (tribes): These units structured economic activity, the operation of power and cultural identification.

Interactions with European explorers, missionaries, sealers, whalers and traders promoted a growing sense on the commonalities that connected Māori in the early nineteenth century, but political authority still resided in rangatira, the chiefly leaders of hapū and iwi. Following the formal colonization of New Zealand in 1840, Māori faced mounting pressure from European colonists to sell their land, while at the same time the growth of the colonial economy, the spread of Christianity, and the embrace of literacy reshaped Māori social organization. In response to these dynamics, Māori leaders deployed a range of strategies to try to secure the future of their communities: A significant number embraced the Christian churches, becoming Methodists, Anglicans or Catholics; others followed the radical new visions of indigenous prophets who claimed the Bible as their own, while rejecting the authority of missionaries and colonial rule; others still focused on strengthening their iwi as the power of their rangatira were undermined and their traditional resource-bases depleted.

Kīngitanga was a distinctive and influential response to the pressures of the colonial order. The leaders of this movement believed that unifying behind a single leader was the best strategy to protect Māori interests in the face of colonialism. In the 1840s and 1850s, some Māori who had traveled to Britain, such as Tāmihana Te Rauparaha (Ngāti Toa), had become influential advocates for a pan-tribal movement unified behind a single leader whose authority would resemble that of the Queen of England.

In the early 1850s, Tāmihana and Mātene Te Whiwhi of Ngāti Raukawa began searching for an appropriate leader, but many influential rangatira responded by stressing their position as tribal leaders. At an important gathering of iwi leaders at Pūkawa in 1856, Iwikau Te Heuheu of Tūwharetoa suggested that the renowned rangatira of the Waikato iwi, Pōtatau Te Wherowhero, should lead the new movement and in the following year Pōtatau accepted this honor.

When Pōtatau assumed the mantle of leading this movement at Ngāruawāhia in 1858 he was called "King." The use of this European term rather than indigenous alternatives grounded in the older language of tribal authority such as Toihau (head chief), Matua (Father or Chief) or Ariki (paramount Chief) marked an important shift in Māori political culture.

Drawing together many of the key North Island tribes, Kīngitanga was an assertion of unity and nationhood. Its authority was not accepted by all tribes, and its key powerbase was in the lands of the Waikato iwi (who became known as the primary guardians of Kīngitanga) and within the traditional lands of Ngāti Maniapoto, which stretched to the west and south toward the North Island's volcanic plateau. In a potent display of the King's authority the followers of Kīngitanga policed an "aukati," a boundary line that demarcated the King's authority and they restricted the flows of goods and the movement of colonists over this border.

Kīngitanga was strongly inflected by Christianity, but it primarily reflected a drive by Māori leaders to carve out a secure and autonomous space within the colonial order. It was underpinned by a desire to halt the alienation of traditional lands and to shore up the social foundations of Māori life. Its leaders stressed the British Queen and law were to be respected, as both derived their authority from God. In fact "the law of God" was seen to join the King and the British Queen in a complementary relationship. The King was responsible for the maintenance of law and order within the aukati (boundary), while the Queen's sovereignty was to be recognized by all, both colonists and Māori beyond the aukati. One of the traditional sayings of Kīngitanga underlined this complementary: "The King on his piece; the Queen on her piece, God over both; and Love binding them to each other."

For many colonists and the colonial state, however, the rise of Kīngitanga marked an unacceptable challenge to British sovereignty, especially in the wake of the war in the Taranaki region in 1860–1861. Governor Gore-Browne and his replacement Governor George Grey worked hard to undermine support for the new King Tāwhiao (who succeeded his father in 1860). Against the backdrop of deepening anxieties over colonial authority, British troops and a significant number of their Māori allies invaded the Waikato with the aim of extinguishing this perceived challenge to the Queen's sovereignty. Deploying deft tactics, Kīngitanga forces frustrated the colonial state, which had superior resources and was able to deploy much larger numbers of soldiers in the field. After the colonial state's repeated attacks on the Kīngitanga stronghold at Ōrākau, many of the surviving supporters of the King fled south into Ngāti Maniapoto lands, which became known as the "King Country."

The colonial government denounced King Tāwhiao and his followers as rebels and confiscated some 1.2 million acres of their land. This "raupatu" (confiscation) not only became a potent grievance for Waikato Māori, but it also enriched colonists who took up these lands. From this powerbase in the King Country, King Tāwhiao argued strongly against violence, but he remained critical of colonial institutions and technologies, advocating for the separation between Māori and colonists. After protracted negotiations, Tāwhiao and his followers were allowed to return to Waikato in 1881.

Successive leaders of Kīngitanga made the movement an enduring feature of Māori political and cultural life. In the twentieth century, Kīngitanga remained an important vehicle for the aspiration for "mana motuhake" (independent authority) and the restitution of confiscated lands. It also became a significant engine for the improvement of Māori land and for securing a stronger and more stable economic base for Māori communities. Increasingly, Kīngitanga worked with the state to achieve these goals (see **N is for Native Claim-making**).

Kīngitanga lives on today. The first female Kīngitanga leader, Queen Dame Te Ātairangikaahu, ruled as Māori Queen for forty years (1966–2006), and she was a highly respected figure in New Zealand public life. Her son Tūheitia Paki was crowned in 2006 and despite ill-health has been prominent in the institutional life of Māori communities, in reinforcing bonds with Pacific island nations, and in building new partnerships between the New Zealand state and Māori communities.

Suggestions for Further Reading

Belich, James. *The New Zealand Wars*. London: Penguin, 1986.

Dalton, B. J. *War and Politics in New Zealand 1855–1870*. Sydney: Sydney University Press, 1967.

Gorst, J. E. *The Maori King: Or, the Story of Our Quarrel with the Natives of New Zealand*. London: Macmillan, 1864.

Walker, Ranginui. *Ka Whawhai Tonu Matou: Struggle Without End*. London: Penguin, 1990.

K is also for . . .

Kat River Settlement
Khartoum
Khyber Pass
Kilmainham Jail
Kruger, Paul

L is for Lascar

In this etching from Blanchard Jerrold and Gustave Dore's famous book London: A Pilgrimage (1872), the way that lascars mixed with the rest of London's East End poor is apparent. With upward of 3,000 lascars arriving in British port cities by the mid-1870s, they were not contained to Whitechapel streets like this one, but were part of many Victorian cityscapes. Heritage Images.

If you were a Victorian Londoner or visitor to the capital city and you happened to wander into the East End, you might well imagine that you had stumbled into an extension of the British Empire on metropolitan soil. Here, you might encounter Indians, Africans and Chinese mixed with white working-class men and women in the streets, the boarding houses and the docks. The lascar—or seaman of Indian origin—would likely be prime among them. Defined in the eighteenth century as a native of East India Company territories, lascars were to be found on the streets of London in increasing numbers in the nineteenth century—either because they had jumped ship or were illegally discharged. They were not, of course, the only kinds of "colonials" who made their way to the metropole. People of color, slave and free, had been a feature of the London landscape since early modern times. During the reign of Victoria, Indians and Africans came as travelers, dignitaries, students, laborers and street performers. Though historians have been late to appreciate what a multiracial city London was, contemporaries understood that imperialism sponsored a steady stream of colonial natives seeking their fortune or simply their livelihood at the heart of the empire. This is not to say that Victorians, whether officials or social observers, were happy about the inflow of racialized migrants to the Island Kingdom. Lascars, in particular, were a source of alarm and intervention, even as they represented one face of empire "at home."

In a country with anti-vagrancy laws dating back to the Elizabethan era, the prime concern when it came to lascars was the legitimacy of their claims to residence and permanent settlement. By the mid-nineteenth century, their presence on the streets of London drew the attention of the Church Missionary Society, which opened a Strangers Home for Asiatics, Africans and South Sea Islanders in 1857—both in order to shelter them and to try to repatriate them as well. This was on the heels of a very harsh English winter that saw impoverished lascars dying of cold and hunger on the streets of London. Significantly, among the Home's patrons was the Maharaja of Duleep Singh—a reminder that not all Indians who came to Britain were down and out (see **G is for Gandhi**). As well, by the nineteenth century, not all lascars were technically people of South Asian descent; or, rather, the question of ethnic classification was a murky one, as the title of the 1814–1815 "Report on Lascars and other Asiatic Seamen" suggests. As part of the city's destitute—what Victorian social reformers referred to as the residuum—lascars were often lumped with Poles, Arabs and "negroes" whose racial, ethnic, religious and linguistic differences appeared to blur together in a seamless continuum of colonial otherness. Joseph Salter, whose 1873 book *Sketches of Sixteen Years' Work Among Orientals*, testified to the tremendous diversity of the term *lascar* as he reported on his travels and encounters with men in London, Glasgow and Cardiff who were technically counted as such, but whose backgrounds were varied (from Yemen to China, India, Africa and the Pacific Islands, for example).

Regardless of their heterogeneous origins, lascars provoked suspicion and anxiety, mainly because of the association of lascars with opium smoking and other activities the Victorians considered vices (see **O is for Opium**). Bracebridge Heming, a popular novelist and urban sleuth, gave this account of his tour of "low lodging-houses" in the East End of London with one Inspector Price (32):

The house was a wretched tumble-down hovel, and the poor woman complained bitterly that her landlord would make no repairs. The first room we entered contained a Lascar, who had come over in some vessel, and his woman. There was a sickly smell in the chamber, that I discovered proceeded from the opium he had been smoking. There was not a chair to be seen; nothing but a table, upon which were placed a few odds and ends. The Lascar was lying on a palliasse placed upon the floor (there was no bedstead), apparently stupefied from the effects of the opium he had been taking. A couple of old tattered blankets sufficed to cover him. By his bedside sat a woman, who was half idiotically endeavoring to derive some stupefaction from the ashes he had left in his pipe. Her face was grimy and unwashed, and her hands so black and filthy that mustard-and-cress might have been sown successfully upon them. As she was huddled up with her back against the wall she appeared an animated bundle of rags. She was apparently a powerfully made woman, and although her face was wrinkled and careworn, she did not appear decrepit, but more like one thoroughly broken down in spirit than in body. In all probability she was diseased; and the disease communicated by the Malays, Lascars and Orientals generally is said to be the most frightful form of lues [i.e., syphilis] to be met with in Europe. It goes by the name of Dry—, and is much dreaded by all the women in the neighborhood of the docks.

Here, all of the Victorians' fears of the lascar as alien converge: stupefaction via opium and venereal disease as a result of contact with equally alien women (see **S is for Syphilis**). The passage is significant for its preoccupation with the lascar's wife, of whom there is less visual or archival trace in the Victorian record than the lascar himself. She is rendered not simply as foreign, but also as scarcely human" so "black" with dirt she could serve as soil for growing garden cress and so tattered that she resembled a bundle of rags. Heming is eager to persuade readers that it's the lascar's penchant for opium that is responsible for her condition, though she has agency as well: for she is the carrying of sexual contagion, a threat to both the East End and—if she is a prostitute—to the nation at large (see **S is for Syphilis**). Lascars were both a regular feature of the urban landscape and a reminder to

Victorians of the ways that empire could come home, bringing with it both a richly multicultural community and anxieties about the impact of colonial practices and bodies on the "native" society and culture of Britain.

Selections for Further Reading

Jaffer, Aaron. *Lascars and Indian Ocean Seafaring, 1780–1860*. Suffolk: Boydell, 2015.

Lahiri, Shompa. *Indians in Britain: Anglo-Indian Encounters, Race and Identity, 1880–1930*. London: Routledge 2013.

Lindeborg, Ruth H. The "Asiatic" and the Boundaries of Victorian Englishness, *Victorian Studies* 37, 3 (1994): 381–404.

Salter, Joseph. *The Asiatic in England: Sketches of Sixteen Years' Work Among Orientals*. London: Seeley, Jackson and Halliday, 1873.

Seddon, Mohammed Siddique. *The Last of the Lascars: Yemeni Muslims in Britain, 1836–2012*. Leicestershire: Kube Publishing, 2014.

Visram, Rozina. *Ayahs, Lascars and Princes: The Story of Indians in Britain, 1700–1947*. London: Pluto, 1986.

L is also for . . .

Ladies National Association
Lancashire cotton mills
Land League
Laylor, James Fenton
Lugard, Lord Frederick

M is for Morant Bay

The power of the crowd, and of people of African descent, in the Morant Bay Rebellion can be seen vividly in this rendering of the attack on the courthouse in St.-Thomas-the-East parish in October 1865. Culture Club, October 11, 1865.

Morant Bay, which is in the parish of St. Thomas on the eastern side of the island of Jamaica, was the site of a popular rebellion in 1865 that cost hundreds of lives and the reputation of an English colonial governor. The events at "Bloody Bay," as it came to be known, reverberated from the local town hall to Whitehall—reminding Victorians in the metropole and the colony that subjects of the Queen were willing to take up arms against the representatives of colonial authority on the spot. The Morant Bay rebellion was brutally suppressed by the Governor Edward Eyre, whose imposition of martial law and summary execution of several prominent Jamaican rebels caused a firestorm in Britain. He was recalled from the island and charged with murder more than once, though the cases against him were unsuccessful. Morant Bay earned Eyre the nickname "the monster of Jamaica" and raised the specter of imperial disorder as a problem not just for the colony, but for metropolitan politics as well.

Paul Bogle was the deacon of Stony Gut Baptist Church who organized blacks on a march to the Morant Bay courthouse to address their grievances in October 1865. They brandished sticks, cutlasses, and according to one witness, arms they had taken from a police station on their way into town. At the front of the group was Letitia Geoghagan, who "fired a stone," upon which other women followed suit, "and then the men rushed in" (Sheller, 127). Though the original cause of the protest was a series of warrants taken out against Stony Gut villagers in a case that involved trespassing on a plantation, Bogle was able to galvanize local protesters around a number of pressing issues. Economic conditions on the island had been deteriorating since the abolition of slavery and the institution of indenture in the 1830s (Heuman). What's more, black Jamaicans were frustrated by their political disenfranchisement: Though they were a majority population, their voting rights were limited and their interests were not represented in the Assembly. Rumors that whites planned to bring back slavery were rampant. When Bogle and his followers were fired on in their attempts to seek redress at the courthouse, the rebellion was launched.

Bogle led the call to arms, announcing it is now time for us to help ourselves—skin to skin. The iron bar is now broken in this parish.... Every one of you must leave your house. Take your guns; who don't have guns take your cutlasses at once. Blow your shells, roal [*sic*] your drums house to house to house.... War is at us, my black skin. War is at hand. (Holt, 262)

The protesters-turned-rioters roamed the region, targeting specific individuals, mostly whites, and evoking the image of the Haitian revolution for English residents who understood the racial demography of the island and their own vulnerability. Eyre described Jamaica as being "on the brink of a volcano" and authorized the ruthless pursuit of the rebels. As one soldier recalled, "We slaughtered all before us ... man or woman or child." More than 400 blacks were killed, and flogging was the punishment of choice for those arrested and imprisoned on suspicion of sedition. Letitia, her sons and countless others were publicly executed as an example to those who remained.

George William Gordon, a mixed-race Assemblyman, a landowner in his own right and a political associate of Paul Bogle, had been vocal in his criticism of Governor Eyre, whom he held responsible for the poor conditions of the island's black population. Though there is little evidence that he was actively involved in the rebellion itself, he was popular as "the poor man's friend"—and he was not intimidated by the initial show of government force. A week after Bogle's march on the courthouse, he openly blamed Eyre for causing the uprising in the first place: "... when the Governor and his advisors take upon themselves to make their will the law of the land, and that law is cruelly obnoxious to the people ... the lower classes become equally callous on their part and riotous in their way. A Governor that sows the wind must expect to real the whirlwind" (Sheller, 123). Eyre was determined to suppress those who led the rebellion whether in the street or through the pen. Gordon was arrested, tried under martial law and executed, as were Paul Bogle and his brother William, all within two weeks of the initial march on the courthouse.

Eyre had been Lieutenant Governor of New Zealand, and before that, an explorer in southern and western Australia. Though initially praised by the Liberal government in Britain, his actions came under further scrutiny as word of the reprisals spread through the metropolitan press and the humanitarian community at home. A Royal Commission was called to investigate and the witness testimony that the commissioners collected remains the major archive for understanding how events in Morant Bay unfolded. The political theorist and Member of Parliament John Stuart Mill called for a trial on the grounds that Eyre's excesses had resulted in the murder of British subjects. With the support of both liberal and radical men of the day, from Charles Darwin to Herbert Spencer, he formed the Jamaica Committee to seek Eyre's prosecution. Though Liberal anger did not preclude some sympathy for Eyre's predicament, it polarized public opinion nonetheless. One result was the creation of the Eyre Defense Fund, championed by the Victorian conservative thinker Thomas Carlyle—who managed to raise considerable sums in support of the governor. As important, the two campaigns generated heated debate in Britain about the nature of the colonial rule of law, the status of "negro" civilization and the tendency of blacks toward rebellion, and the proper role of the Englishman in keeping political order. Nor were English women silent. Though some supported Mill, many were also involved in the Eyre Defence Fund, supporting in word and deed the forms of civilized English masculinity over black barbarism that Carlyle himself advocated (Hall).

These debates, which revolved not just around the legitimacy of Eyre's actions, but also around the capacity of blacks to participate in democratic forms of political participation of the kind that George William Gordon embodied, catalyzed larger arguments about the racial character of good government that lasted well beyond the fate of Eyre was decided. As tempting as it is to see the events of Morant Bay in black and white, in fact, it's more complex than that. Gordon himself was the son a of a Scottish planter and a slave; poor whites had some of the same economic grievances as black rebels; the Maroon community on the island helped suppress the rebellion; and some black Jamaicans supported the Eyre Defence Fund. Meanwhile, in Jamaica, the rebel dead were buried in mass graves and an eye witness testified that soldiers had taken Gordon's effects—coat, vest and spectacles—"as a prize" (Sheller, 122). Not only were rebels shot, but houses and farms were also burned, leaving the Morant Bay end of the island scarred in the long and short run by the rebellion and the counter-insurgency both. In 1965, a statute evoking the image of Paul Bogle was installed in front of the courthouse in Morant Bay to commemorate the centenary of the Jamaican rebellion (see also image in **X is for Xhosaland**). Today, Paul Bogle is considered a Jamaican national hero, and Morant Bay remains a matter of lively national conversation and historical memory.

Suggestions for Further Reading

Berry, Francis. *Morant Bay and Other Poems*. London: Routledge and Kegan Paul, 1961.

Hall, Catherine. *White Male and Middle-Class: Explorations in Feminism and History*. London: Polity Press, 1992.

Heuman, Gad. *The Killing Time: Morant Bay Rebellion in Jamaica*. Knoxville: University of Tennessee Press, 1995.

Holt, Thomas. *The Problem of Freedom: Race, Labor and Politics in Jamaica in Britain*. Baltimore: Johns Hopkins University Press, 1991.

Sheller, Mimi. *Citizenship from Below: Erotic Agency and Caribbean Freedom*. Durham: Duke University Press, 2012.

Winter, Sarah. "On the Morant Bay Rebellion in Jamaica and the Governor Eyre-George William Gordon Controversy, 1865–70," *BRANCH: Britain, Representation and Nineteenth-Century History*. Ed. Dino Franco Felluga. Extension of *Romanticism and Victorianism on the Net*. Web. Last accessed November 2015.

M is also for . . .

Malakand Field Force
Maori Wars
Martial law
Matabeleland
Miscegenation

N is for Native Claim-making

A scene from the battle at Cawnpore (Kanpur), where an entire British garrison, including women and children, was wiped out during the Indian Mutiny, 1857. This battle was one of the most well-known instances of native claim-making in the whole Victorian empire. Hulton Archive.

Native claim-making was a recurrent practice across the wide expanses of Victoria's colonial possessions precisely because territorial expansion was a characteristic feature of British imperialism in the nineteenth century. That expansion entailed the conquest of lands belonging to indigenous people, along with the abrogation of their rights not just *to* possession, but *as* sovereign communities as well. Histories of the nineteenth-century empire tend to emphasize a rise-and-fall narrative, a story in which empire started tenuously, gained ground and began to experience structural crisis—the latter typically at the century's end, in the debacle of the Boer War, which the British won but at great cost in soldiers and psychic certainty about their long-range hegemonic ambitions. Yet, indigenous people were not simply (or easily) overtaken by their would-be British masters. They staged resistance at spectacular moments of conquest or crisis, as in the Indian Mutiny (see **T is for Tatya Tope**) or the British occupation of Egypt (see **U is for Urabi**). They also chipped away on a regular basis at whatever semi-permanent settlements followed in the wake of presumptive British victories, creating a fragile and precarious terrain of empire that was as defense against native claims at a variety of scales as it was aggressive in the face of the prospect of expansion and extension. The story of nineteenth-century imperialism is thus a history of dissent and disruption rather than of empire ascendant, as the regular assertion of indigenous pushback testifies. Claims made by native people and communities in various forms and idioms is key to appreciating the challenges faced by those in charge of extending and maintaining Victoria's empire.

In part because land was the biggest resource at issue at moments of conquest and negotiation, native claims were most often legal in nature. Treaty making was a distinctive feature of British imperial settlement from the colony at Jamestown to the Treaty of Waitangi negotiated with Māori in 1840. Though "empire by treaty" implies a diplomatic negotiation that fixes boundaries and ends military conflict over land and sovereignty, treaties were most often starting points for decades of contest and even future war. Though their origins were complex—bound up in the urgency of providing land to European immigrants and in Māori resistance to the Crown's monopoly on land sales—the New Zealand wars of the 1840s–1870s testify to the precarious vulnerability of apparently settled treaty principles (see **K is for Kīngitanga**). Of course, native land claims need not rise to the level of war in order to put pressure on the marketizing forces of the British colonial state. In nineteenth-century Lagos, for example, the sale of land accelerated after annexation in 1861, but natives were constantly in the courts, seeking the resolution of disputes with respect to their own law or custom (Mann, 237) and pressing the claim of family as opposed to individual ownership (239). The links between such native claim-making and resistance to British imperialism per se were so tight that a victory in court was seen as a powerful political (i.e., anticolonial) statement as well (240).

Native claim-making took a variety of forms, the boycott among the most collectively driven and symbolically powerful of them. The term was coined in 1880s Ireland in the context of protests against Captain Charles Boycott, a British land agent in County Mayo. Local adherents to the Irish Land League program—which was designed to restore native Irish claims to Irish soil—displayed their objection to his tenant practices, withheld custom on his local shops and effectively hampered his capacity to exercise his authority in situ. As he bemoaned in a letter to *The Times*, "I can get no workmen to do anything, and my ruin is openly avowed as the object of the Land League unless I throw up everything and leave the country." Though we tend to associate the boycott practice with twentieth-century spectacles of resistance to empire, in fact, it has untold nineteenth-century histories. As early as the 1860s, Bengali nationalists organized the *mela*, or fair, to promote the manufacture of home-made goods, and by extension, to substitute them for British-made materials. This laid the groundwork for later movements to boycott British manufactures, most famously in the Partition of Bengal in 1905–1906. But again, there were Victorian precedents. In the 1870s, Bholanath Chandra called for Indians to resolve to "nonconsume the goods of England," and thus, to "dethrone

King Cotton of Manchester" (quoted in Burton, 99). Boycotting is admittedly a kind of negative affirmation: a claim that's made through withdrawal or withholding. Yet, its agency is clear: It acknowledges that economic power is at the heart of the imperial relationship; it recognizes colonial subjects as holders of that power; and it asserts a claim over the very terms by which market governance is to proceed— or not—in daily forms of imperial exchange and encounter.

Claims for native sovereignty and power were also made much more vociferously in Victoria's empire, chiefly through war or rebellion. The Irish used a diasporic strategy to try to reclaim the nation from British occupation via Fenian violence (see **B is for Bold Fenian Men**) and republican insurgency (see **P is for the Proclamation of the Irish Republic**). The Indian Mutiny was certainly an expression of determination that the subcontinent be delivered from British rule and returned to natives—though the quest to restore the Mughal kingdom of Delhi complicated the question of who, under the Raj, was indigenous and who was simply an earlier occupier. Urabi's origins (he was the son of a headman) gave his revolution (see **U is for Urabi**) a nativist cast, and the two successive Afghan Wars suggest that, despite treaties that appeared to settling native claims, settlement, in fact, was elusive at worst, and tenuous at best (see **A is for the Afghan Wars**). There are numerous large- and small-scale challenges to British imperial hegemony animated by indigenous conviction that colonial rule was neither inevitable nor fully or finally accomplished in the Victorian period. In that sense, Pax Britannica was a nineteenth-century fiction, albeit a powerful one.

Selections for Further Reading

Burton, Antoinette. *The Trouble with Empire: Challenges to Modern British Imperialism.* New York: Oxford University Press, 2015.

Belmessous, Saliha. *Empire by Treaty: Negotiating European Expansion, 1600–1900*. New York: Oxford University Press, 2014.

Harris, Cole. *Making Native Space: Colonialism, Resistance, and Reserves in British Columbia*. Vancouver: University of British Columbia Press, 2003.

Ritter, David. *Contesting Native Title: From Controversy to Consensus in the Struggle over Indigenous Land Rights*. London: Allen and Unwin, 2009.

Simpson, Audra. *Theorizing Native Studies*. Durham: Duke University Press, 2014.

Veracini, Lorenzo. *Settler Colonialism: A Theoretical Overview*. Palgrave Macmillan, 2010.

N is also for . . .

Neill, Lieutenant Colonel James
Nongqawuse
Nonviolence
Norman Commission
Northwest Provinces

O is for Opium

The Opium Wars were a battle for Asian markets at a moment when Victorian imperialism was unfolding in both chaotic and plural ways. Though Chinese were often viewed as monstrously "oriental" by British commentators, this image reminds us of how alien Europeans looked to their Chinese "enemies" as well. Hulton Archive—Illustrated London News.

Opium preoccupied the Victorians as both a question of social morality and a threat to imperial security (see also **D is for Dagga**). Britain fought two wars with China over it; an anti-opium movement thrived for almost half a century; and Charles Dickens thrilled readers with images of an opium den in *The Mystery of Edwin Drood*, which Gustave Dore then materialized in his 1872 *London, A Pilgrimage*. Evocative of dangerous "oriental" passions and fundamental to the finances of Britain's eastern empire, opium drove geopolitical decisions with global consequences. Yet, it was also a quite ordinary and readily available drug in nineteenth-century Britain, given regularly as laudanum to infants or small children to cure colic or a toothache, and recommended in a variety of cures. Godfrey's Cordial and McMunn's Elixir both contained admixtures of various opiate derivatives and were advertised and sold as prescriptions for nerves or convulsions. And while those calling for its ban were by far the most vociferous, there were some who thought that Britons would be far better off eating or drinking opium than consuming alcohol because it was cheaper, and in moderation, better for health. Known for its sedative properties, opium animated local, regional, national and imperial debates across the whole of the Victorian period.

The British famously went to war with the Qing dynasty in 1839 over opium revenues, in part because Chinese objections to the flow of the drug threatened the profits of the East India Company, which oversaw its cultivation, mainly in Bengal. Commissioner Liz Xenu confiscated several hundred tons of the stuff, and the British were determined to avenge this unprecedented, and in their view unwarranted, seizure. The war concluded in 1842 with the Treaty of Nanking, which established five treaty ports, and most significantly for the long-term world order, ceded Hong Kong to the British for a term of 150 years. By 1856, the British and the Chinese were at war again, once more over opium but also over a broader set of issues about Britain's privileged status as first among equals vis-à-vis various foreign powers now seeking commercial exchange with the Qing. This second war had several phases, saw the French ally with the

British and concluded with a spectacular conflagration: the burning of the Summer Palaces in Peking in the wake of the emperor's flight.

Revenues from opium were a high-stakes game well beyond the second Chinese defeat: Between 1840 and 1899, they amounted to over six million rupees, which represented fully 15 percent of all Indian revenue (Richards). There were some in Victorian Britain, certainly, who objected to this kind of monopoly. But as with other forms of British imperial profit, the opium trade was justified through civilizing rhetoric, most of which was focused on the corrosive effects of opium addiction on the Chinese, who some missionaries and other reformers believed were being eaten away, literally and figuratively, by their consumption of the drug. Such poison, they argued, was unworthy of an Imperial parliament and the trusteeship over lesser races with which it had been entrusted. Others were clearer-headed. As William Lawson put it in 1886, "It came to this, that by hook or crook, money must be had to fight Russia, or to steal rubies from Burma; and so it has to be got by poisoning the Chinese, and then we thanked God we were not as other nations." Opium profits were, in other words, the price that had to be paid for imperial ambition and hegemony.

The specter of the opium addict was a popular feature of the domestic urban scene as well, thanks in part to Charles Dickens. Opium appears as a killer and an agent of madness in *Bleak House* and *The Mystery of Edwin Drood,* respectively (see also **L is for Lascar**). In the character of John Jasper, readers could see the fine line between legal and illegal drug use; they were drawn into the dark, grim precincts of the opium den; and they could apprehend the consequences of oriental culture and practices on English culture and society at home—namely, transformation from one "state" to another and from respectable citizen to criminal deviant. Dickens himself was, incidentally, a casual consumer of opium via laudanum, though this was not the only basis for his representations of it in his novels. He did some slumming with local policemen in Shadwell as part of his research for the opening scenes of the book; in so doing, he helped to solidify the association between London's East End and an Orientalized East at the very heart of the empire. By the end of his life, Dickens' use of laudanum had accelerated; he was using it to treat pain in his foot, and there has been speculation that he may have actually died of an overdose from the drug rather than from a massive heart attack as reported (Polsky). Ironically, his untimely death prevented him from finishing *Edwin Drood*.

Nor was Dickens the only popularizer of lurid images that Victorians came to associate with excessive opium use. Wilkie Collins was a well-known opium abuser. The protagonist in his novel *The Moonstone*, Ezra Jennings, is an opium addict who is widely believed to be a largely autobiographical character. His nightly terrors are vividly conveyed in the following passage:

> June 16th.—Rose late, after a dreadful night; the vengeance of yesterday's opium, pursuing me through a series of frightful dreams. At one time I was whirling through empty space with the phantoms of the dead, friends and enemies together. At another, the one beloved face which I shall never see again, rose at my bedside, hideously phosphorescent in the black darkness, and glared and grinned at me. A slight return of the old pain, at the usual time in the early morning, was welcome as a change. It dispelled the visions—and it was bearable because it did that.

Sherlock Holmes was famously portrayed as working incognito in a London opium den in Arthur Conan Doyle's short story, "The Man with the Twisted Lip"—a hint of the darker addiction to heroin that was to come. But it was arguably the Society for the Suppression of the Opium Trade and its advocates that did the most to keep the image of the dissolute opium smoker before the British public. The Society flooded the late Victorian periodical press with propaganda about Chinese objections to the drugs importation as well as attacks on the propriety of the Indian revenue connection. An 1880 Royal Commission reported on the problem, but despite all attempts to publicize the "truth" about opium smoking, it was not banned until 1913.

Suggestions for Further Reading

Collins, Wilkie. *The Moonstone*. London: Penguin Classics, 1999.

Dore, Gustave. *London, A Pilgrimage*. London: Dover Publications, 1970.

Milligan, Barry. *Pleasures and Pains: Opium and the Orient in Nineteenth-Century British Culture*. Charlottesville: University Press of Virginia, 1995.

Mills, James, and Patricia Barton, eds. *Essays in Modern Imperialism and Intoxication, c. 1500 to c. 1930*. London: Palgrave Macmillan, 2007.

Polsky, Stephanie. "The Novel Ingestion of Opium and Orientalism in *The Mystery of Edwin Drood*," *The Victorian* 3, 1 (2015).

Richards, J. F. "The Indian Empire and Peasant Production of Opium in the Nineteenth Century," *Modern Asian Studies* 15, 1 (1981): 59–82.

O is also for . . .

O'Connell, Daniel
Omdurman
Orange Free State
Order of Orangemen
Oudh

P is for the Proclamation of the Irish Republic

FENIANS TAKING POSSESSION OF ST. ARMAND.

Fenianism was a revolutionary movement with transnational ambitions in the 1860s and beyond. From North America to Australia, Irish republicans had symbols of British imperial power in their sights, and high hopes for a Fenian take-over. None, including the invasion of St. Armand in Canada in June 1866, pictured here, was ultimately successful.

On March 4, 1867, *The Times* of London received a document entitled "Proclamation!" which was addressed from "The Irish People to the World" and signed "The Provisional Government." It read as follows:

We have suffered centuries of outrage, enforced poverty, and bitter misery. Our rights and liberties have been trampled on by an alien aristocracy, who treating us as foes, usurped our lands, and drew away from our unfortunate country all material riches. The real owners of the soil were removed to make room for cattle, and driven across the ocean to seek the means of living, and the political rights denied to them at home, while our men of thought and action were condemned to loss of life and liberty. But we never lost the memory and hope of a national existence. We appealed in vain to the reason and sense of justice of the dominant powers.

Our mildest remonstrances were met with sneers and contempt. Our appeals to arms were always unsuccessful.

Today, having no honourable alternative left, we again appeal to force as our last resource. We accept the conditions of appeal, manfully deeming it better to die in the struggle for freedom than to continue an existence of utter serfdom.

All men are born with equal rights, and in associating to protect one another and share public burdens, justice demands that such associations should rest upon a basis which maintains equality instead of destroying it.

We therefore declare that, unable longer to endure the curse of Monarchical Government, we aim at founding a Republic based on universal suffrage, which shall secure to all the intrinsic value of their labour.

The soil of Ireland, at present in the possession of an oligarchy, belongs to us, the Irish people, and to us it must be restored.

We declare, also, in favour of absolute liberty of conscience, and complete separation of Church and State.

We appeal to the Highest Tribunal for evidence of the justness of our cause. History bears testimony to the integrity of our sufferings, and we declare, in the face of our brethren, that we intend no war against the people of England—our war is against the aristocratic locusts, whether English or Irish, who have eaten the verdure of our fields—against the aristocratic leeches who drain alike our fields and theirs.

Republicans of the entire world, our cause is your cause. Our enemy is your enemy. Let your hearts be with us. As for you, workmen of England, it is not only your hearts we wish, but your arms. Remember the starvation and degradation brought to your firesides by the oppression of labour. Remember the past, look well to the future, and avenge yourselves by giving liberty to your children in the coming struggle for human liberty.

The proclamation was intended as the founding statement of the would-be Irish Republic: the political manifesto of a revolutionary government sponsored by the Fenians (see **B is for Bold Fenian Men**), who sought to challenge British rule in Ireland. Among the Fenians' supporters in Ireland were artisans and school teachers, laborers and small shopkeepers—tailors, ironworkers, messengers, clerks, bricklayers, weavers, dyers and porters: a considerable and representative slice, in other words, of the Irish working class. By autumn of 1864, they were said to number 54,000 and to have 8,000 recruits in the British army in Ireland and abroad.

Yet, despite their size and years of planning, including the steady shipment of American arms, the much-anticipated 1865 rebellion had not occurred (see also **B is for Bold Fenian Men**). The British government carried out preemptive raids, including on the offices of the *Irish People*, the short-lived Fenian newspaper. James Stephens, an Irish Repubican Brotherhood (IRB) founder and one of its main architects, was arrested and jailed. The Fenians broke Stephens out of Richmond jail and got him into hiding—an act of daring that sent the British authorities scrambling in anticipation of an uprising that they believed could erupt anywhere in Britain. Fearing the symbolism of St. Patrick's Day 1866, the British purged the army of suspected Fenians via 150 court-martials, suspended habeas corpus and undertook a massive dragnet, detaining more than 700 without trial.

Though these tactics created serious challenges for the IRB, 1866 was nonetheless a year of tremendous upheaval in Britain proper, and Stephens was determined to cultivate allies through *sub rosa* connections and in legitimate political circles. In July, the Reform League, which sought to extend the franchise to the working classes, held demonstrations in Hyde Park, which had the police on the defensive, and in the words of one observer, had the makings of "desperate deeds and revolution" (Newsinger, 51). Stephens made overtures to British radicals even as he continued to cultivate transatlantic alliances, including with the agent of the International Working Men's Association in New York. Meanwhile, the provisional government of the Irish Republic was established in secrecy off the Tottenham Court Road (London), and its Proclamation was issued in February 1867. With its direct address to "the Irish People of the World" and its unflinching claim on Irish territorial sovereignty ("the soil of Ireland, at present in the possession of an oligarchy, belongs to us, the Irish people, and to us it must be restored"), the Proclamation was a call to arms as well as an announcement of republican intention. It was also a declaration of political war on the British Empire at home.

The Fenian rising, called for March 5, was a notorious failure. Despite minor, short-lived successes in Kerry and Dublin, plans for an all-out rebellion fell disastrously short. In Britain, an attempt to storm the castle at Chester also failed. Britons following the drama would have been most riveted by the so-called "Manchester martyrs"— William Philip Allen, Michael Larkin and Michael O'Brien—whose attempts to free IRB prisoners resulted in the killing of a policeman and their swift arrest. The Manchester Irish were terrorized when the police raided their quarters in an attempt to hunt them out; following their conviction they were hanged in short order outside of New Bailey prison in Salford in November 1867. The British press sent up a chorus calling for "retribution swift and stern." Panic about Fenian terrorism was generally all over Britain, and the specter of a republican Ireland was in everyone's sights.

As the text of the proclamation suggests, Irish republicanism was an international movement with global ambition ("Republicans of the entire world, our cause is your cause. Our enemy is your enemy. Let your hearts be with us"). But it was deeply rooted in the class war against British imperialism, with its emphasis on the alienation of land and labor, and its call for universal suffrage—a heated topic in England in 1867, when the Second Reform Act was debated and ultimately passed, granting the vote to only the aristocrats of labor and excluding women in the process. Though broken by the execution of its leaders, Irish radicals continued to target British interests on British soil: that is, to bring its claims about the illegitimacy of British rule directly to the sightline of Britons at home. Though it originated in the context of Victorian imperialism, the republican threat and its associated manifestations remained an irritant, and a menacing one, in one form or the other until the Easter Rising of 1916 and the formation of the Irish Free State in 1922—and beyond.

Suggestions for Further Reading

Jenkins, Brian. *The Fenian Problem: Insurgency and Terrorism in a Liberal State, 1858–1874*. Montreal: McGill-Queen's University Press, 2008.

Moody, T. W. *Davitt and Irish Revolution, 1846–82*. Oxford: Clarendon Press, 1981.

Nelson, Bruce. *Irish Nationalists and the Making of the Irish Race*. Princeton: Princeton University Press, 2012.

Newsinger, John. *The Blood Never Dried: A People's History of the British Empire* London: Bookmarks, 2006.

P is also for . . .

Pan-African Congress
Paramatta factory tirls
Parnell, Charles Stewart
Pathans
Plantation system

Q is for Queensland Sugar

The profits to be made from Queensland sugar meant that imported labor from the Pacific Islands had to be drafted. Among those "recruited" were the women pictured here at Cairns in 1895. Though key to the local economy, their presence was seen as a direct threat to the aspirational whiteness of the region and of Australia as a whole. Queensland State Library.

Queensland sugar denotes a place and product that were mutually steeped in the ideological, economic and social forces that defined the Victorian Empire. In 1885, the Imperial Federationist Harold Finch-Hatton wrote for a British reading public of life in the Australian settler colony of Queensland, and of the tensions that gripped a small sugar-growing town, Mackay. In early 1884, he wrote, groups of armed white men patrolled the streets, police reinforcements were requested from nearby towns and the sales of revolvers and ammunition rose dramatically as the town's white men and women armed themselves with muskets, pistols and butcher's knives (Finch-Hatton, 1885: 166–167). Most were convinced that an uprising was imminent among the town's thousands of indentured plantation workers, imported from the Pacific Islands and called "Kanakas" at the time (see **I is for Indenture**).

The uprising never came, but the anxiety on Mackay's streets encapsulates the enduring imperial dilemma faced by "white"-settler colonies where racial difference was simultaneously relied on and reviled. This was exacerbated in Queensland, which was located deep in the tropics. As the Queensland Attorney General put it in 1895, Queensland was the only colony on "the whole of God's earth" to have attempted "the most difficult problem the World has ever had before it ... the settlement of a tropical country with a purely white race" (*Queensland Parliamentary Debates*, 7).

Queensland matured into a self-governing settler colony in 1859, and its economic future had been envisaged as being based partly in pastoralism and mostly in the production of tropical produce such as sugarcane or cotton. The demand for sugar was insatiable in the Victorian era, and in Britain, its consumption had increased 900 percent between 1830 and 1890 (Walvin, 24). But the production of sugarcane and the refining of it into sugar for mass consumption was still labor-intensive, requiring hundreds of workers to harvest and manage vast plantations and work in pre-industrial refining mills. For centuries, slavery had fuelled the growth of sugar production in the Caribbean, ensuring its economic viability, and by the 1860s, it was still overwhelmingly produced by enslaved and indentured people of color. Free labor, let alone white labor, in the production of sugar was virtually unheard of.

The association of tropical industries with racialized and unfree labor regimes produced an acute labor shortage in Queensland. For white bodies, it was widely believed at the time, were ill-suited to the rigors of physical labor in tropical conditions. It was an assumption based less on science and more on precedent. In 1863, aspiring colonist Robert Towns imported and indentured numerous Pacific Island laborers to work his Queensland plantation. He wrote publicly to the colony's Colonial Secretary George Bowen justifying the development and arguing that this "industrious, tractable, and inoffensive race" of Islanders would "save us from the *inhumanity* of driving to the exposed labor of field work, the less tropically hardy European women and children" (Towns, 2–3).

By 1868, and until 1906, the Queensland government legalized and regulated the use of indentured Pacific Islanders from Melanesia on the colony's canefields, ensuring the economic viability of the industry. At the time, traders servicing the bonded labor needs of white planters in Fiji, New Caledonia, Peru, Samoa, Hawai'i, and later, Papua and New Guinea extensively recruited Melanesians, who were sometimes referred to as Oceanic Negros. In total, more than 60,000 went to Queensland, where they worked for at least three years bonded to their employer for a nominal wage of six pounds per year. The harsh physical labor and conditions on the plantations ensured that Islanders' mortality rates in Queensland were never less than five times the rate of white colonists (Banivanua Mar, 131–132).

Queensland's soon booming sugar industry and the Pacific labor trade that enabled it went on to reflect and epitomize the complex anxieties that accompanied the expansion of Victoria's empire. The use of forced plantation labor was widely condemned by missionaries and humanitarians who saw Islander field gangs as nothing more than barely disguised slave gangs (see **M is for Morant Bay**). The most prominent opposition to the use of black labor, however, came from British colonists concerned about the implications of introducing thousands of black men into what was envisaged as a white-settler colony. This anxiety was at the forefront of the tensions in 1884 in Mackay where the black male population outnumbered the white male population by almost four to one.

Racial tension was never far from the surface in Queensland, and occasionally, erupted into violence. Islanders were portrayed in newspapers, parliamentary debates and published materials as kanaka "boys," who were passive, infantile, pliable servants when safely confined by an indenture contract and the plantations. But when Islanders' period of indenture expired, or they left the plantations and entered white towns as many did in Mackay on Boxing Day in 1883, they were portrayed as a "kanaka menace," as drunk, insolent, violent, savage and dangerous. In Mackay, attempts to contain and discipline the Islanders who came to town on Boxing Day erupted in a fatal brawl. Islanders fought with bottles and sticks against the stirrup irons, horses and guns of the town's white men, and an unknown number of Islanders were killed and later buried in the clammy humidity of the canefields that radiated for miles from the town. This was the incident that sparked the armed tensions that Finch-Hatton later wrote about (see **H is for Hosay**).

The threat that Islanders were seen to pose, or the anxiety that they provoked among Queensland's colonists, was only rarely so immediate and articulate as the seemingly imminent uprising in Mackay. Far more often, it was an indefinite almost existential anxiety. Their blackness and presence, and the colony's reliance on them, destabilized an empire-wide notion of whiteness, and specifically, an emerging British settler identity. By the end of the nineteenth century, Queenslanders and other Australian colonists saw and defined themselves as belonging to a unified white country whose so-called White Australia Policy after 1901 would defend its borders from the rising tide and "Menace of Colour" that surrounded it (Gregory). In this context, Islanders were portrayed as a threat to national purity and their very presence was seen to undermine the perceived virility of this "White Man's Country" (Lake and Reynolds).

By the end of Queen Victoria's reign, mechanization in the sugar industry had replaced the field gangs, and white labor was doing all but the most menial work in the industry. White labor bounties paid planters more for sugar harvested by white labor, and after Queensland joined the federation of Australian colonies in 1901, the new federal government forcibly deported most of the 10,000 Pacific Islanders still resident in the sugar districts. This determination to excise Pacific Islanders from the history of white Queensland spoke clearly of the carefully guarded self-perception that British settlers had cultivated in the permanent colonies of Victoria's empire.

Suggestions for Further Reading

Banivanua Mar, T. *Violence and Colonial Dialogue: The Australian-Pacific Indentured Labor Trade.* Honolulu: University of Hawai'i Press, 2007.

Finch-Hatton, Harold. *Advance Australia! An Account of Eight Years Work, Wanderings and Amusements in Queensland, New South Wales, and Victoria.* London: W.H. Allen and Co.,, 1885.

Gregory, J. W. *The Menace of Colour: A Study of the Difficulties Due to the Association of White and Coloured Races, with an Account of Measures Proposed for Their Solution, and Special Reference to White Colonization in the Tropics.* London: Seeley Service, 1925.

Lake, Marilyn, and Henry Reynolds. *Drawing the Global Color Line: White Men's Countries and the International Challenge of Racial Equality.* Cambridge: Cambridge University Press, 2008.

Queensland Parliamentary Debates, Vol. 74. Brisbane: Government Printer, 1895.

Towns, Robert. *South Sea Island Immigration for Cotton Cultivation: A Letter to the Hon. the Colonial Secretary of Queensland.* Sydney: Reading and Wellbanck, 1864.

Walvin, James. "Sugar and the Shaping of Western Culture" in Pal Ahluwalia, Bill Ashcroft and Roger Knight, eds, *White and Deadly: Sugar and Colonialism.* Commack, NY: Nova Science, 1999: 21–31.

Q is also for . . .

Qing dynasty
Quaker boycotts
Queen's Jubilee
Quinine

R is for Riel, Louis

This image, of uncertain date (1869?) shows Louis Riel and the Metis National Committee Provisional Government. This was formed in Red River Settlement in the winter of 1869–70 as part of an successful resistance against the white-settler takeover of the community. Another armed resistance in 1885 would cost Riel and other Indigenous men their lives. Here, Riel and his councillors are pictured with rugged seriousness about their plans to defend Metis communities and governance against an incoming settler order.

If the record of the (London) *Times* is any measure, the British Empire did not think very much about the life of Louis Riel, the Metis politician, leader, writer and teacher. In 1872, the London newspaper reprinted a few pages of William Francis Butler's memoir *The Great*

Lone Land. It described how Riel, three years earlier, had "usurped the dictatorship of the Red River Settlement, in defiance of the English Crown and the authorities of Canada." It was Riel's leadership of the Northwest Resistance of 1885, and the trial and execution in a Regina Saskatchewan gallows that prompted *The Times* to more clearly register him as part of—and a threat to—the British Empire. The newspaper published a potted biography that described Riel as "the leader of the half-breed insurgents in the Canadian North-West" and noted his leadership of the Red River Resistance from 1869 to 1870. *The Times* followed Riel's trial and failed appeal in a Canadian courtroom, describing him as "half-Indian in blood, and wholly Indian in character and sympathies," and explaining his sympathizers as in the thrall of "race-feeling" and "anarchic regard for outlaws." *The Times* pressed the point that Riel was "more than a political criminal," and indeed, a "murderer, and the instigator of murder, foul, wholesale, and pitiless."

Riel was born in 1844 in Red River Settlement, also known as Red River Colony, or less often, the Selkirk Settlement. The variable nomenclature reflects the place's complicated history as an entity within the British Empire. It was located at the meeting of the Red and Assiniboine rivers in the territories of the Cree, Annishinabe, Dakota and Assiniboine peoples. Since 1670, it had been administered as part of Rupertsland, the enormous territory that the private enterprise of the Hudson's Bay Company claimed to rule, on Britain's behalf. Nestled within Rupertsland, Red River Settlement was an expansive, interconnected set of settlements. At least since the late eighteenth century, it was an important site of Metis community. In 1811, Red River was made into a kind of proprietorial colony, but the sporadic arrivals of Scots, Swiss and other European settlers made modest marks on the settlement's demographic makeup. By the time of Riel's childhood, Red River Settlement was an overwhelmingly Metis society. Some of the Red River Metis were primarily English-speaking and Protestant; others, like Riel, were primarily French-speaking and Roman Catholic. In any case, they were a distinct, indigenous people, with particular geographies, economies and cultural practices, and should not be conflated with people of any "mixed" origins (see **N is for Native Claim-making**).

In 1869, Britain "transferred" title for Rupertsland to Canada, the new settler nation formed just two years before. The deal was negotiated more or less as a real estate transaction, with Canada paying roughly $1.5 million. This was a classic bit of imperial sleight of hand that paid no mind to the overwhelmingly indigenous people of Rupertsland. The community of Red River would powerfully and consequently object. In the winter of 1869–1870, the community set up a self-styled "provisional government" under the leadership of a 24-year-old Riel, recently returned from a Jesuitical education in Montreal (see **P is for the Proclamation of the Irish Republic**). The Red River Resistance was, as nineteenth-century armed colonial rebellions go, a success. In 1870, Manitoba entered Canada not as a colony or territory, but as a province with rights to self-government and with recognition of the French language, the Roman Catholic faith and Metis landholding.

But Canada failed to deliver on many provisions of the Manitoba Act and the more substantial understanding of its promises held by Riel and his colleagues. In the years following 1870, Red River became Winnipeg, an ambitious and self-consciously settler city that fancied itself a kind of Chicago of the North. Having lost much of their land, about two-thirds of the Metis moved north and west to the Northwest Territories, modern-day Saskatchewan and Alberta. After years moving around Canada and the United States, Riel was recruited to lead what would become known as the Northwest Rebellion. The group issued a ten-point "Revolutionary Bill of Rights" and formed a provisional government, naming Riel its president and Metis tactician and hunter Gabriel Dumont its military commander. After months of armed conflict, the Northwest Rebellion was crushed by an increasingly bellicose settler state fearful of the havoc that might be wrecked by widespread indigenous resistance. In its aftermath, Riel was hanged and so were six Cree and two Assiniboine warriors. These were the most visible components of a wider crackdown on indigenous communities and resistance, one that ensured that Western Canada would never be the same (see **J is for Jihad** and **K is for Kīngitanga**).

The British Empire did not think very often of Louis Riel, but he, like so many colonial sons and daughters, had sharp and considered things to say about the empire that claimed to rule them. In their failed appeal of the charge of treason, Riel's lawyers argued that the Metis leader was insane. In his eloquent final statement that preceded his execution, Riel argued that it was British authority over his territory was not only illegitimate, but insane: "British civilization which rules today the world, and the British constitution has defined such government as this is which rules the Northwest Territories as irresponsible government, which plainly means that there is no responsibility." If there was no responsibility, he continued, "it is insane." In Canada, memory of Riel's truncated life and his powerful example and words continue to inform alternative visions of what this place might have been if the vexed histories of empire had dealt it and its leaders a different hand.

Suggestions for Further Reading

Andersen, Chris. *"Metis": Race, Recognition and the Struggle for Indigenous Peoplehood.* Vancouver: University of British Columbia Press, 2014.

Bumsted, J. M. *Thomas Scott's Body: And Other Essays on Early Manitoba History.* Winnipeg: University of Manitoba Press, 2000: 11–36.

Carter, Sarah. *Aboriginal People and Colonizers of Western Canada to 1900.* Toronto: University of Toronto Press, 2004.

Gaudry, Adam, and George Stanley. "Louis Riel," *Canadian Encyclopedia,* http://www.thecanadianencyclopedia.ca/en/article/louis-riel. Last accessed November 2015.

Riel, Louis. "Final Statement and Renunciation of Louis Riel," translated and transcribed, http://law2.umkc.edu/faculty/projects/ftrials/riel/rieltrialstatement .html. Last accessed November 15, 2015.

St.-Onge, Nicole, Carolyn Podruchny and Brenda Macdougall, eds. *Contours of a People: Metis Family, Mobility, and History.* Norman: University of Oklahoma Press, 2012.

Thomas, Lewis H. "Louis Riel," *Dictionary of Canadian Biography*, http://www. biographi.ca/en/bio/riel_louis_1844_85_11E.html. Last accessed November 2015.

R is also for . . .

Rangatiratanga
Republicanism
Rorke's Drift, siege of
Rossa, O'Donovan
Ryots

S is for Syphilis

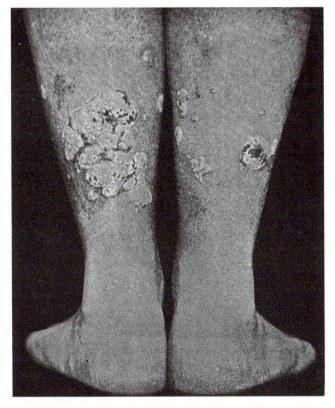

In this graphic image from The Atlas of Syphilis and Venereal Diseases *(1898), some of the physical symptoms of syphilis—a disease considered shameful, even unspeakable—can be seen. Photograph from* The Atlas of Syphilis and Venereal Diseases *by Frank Mracek and Lemuel Bolton Bangs, Vintage Med Stock, 1898.*

Though arguably endemic in Victorian Britain and its empire, syphilis was a disease that dared not speak its name, at least not in polite circles. In his popular novel *Passages from the Diary of a Late Physician*—serialized in the 1830s in *Blackwood's Magazine*—Samuel Warren described a patient's symptoms as follows:

> "It is a peculiar and horrible sensation; and I cannot give you an adequate idea of it," he said; "it is as though the marrow in my bones were transformed into something animated—into blind-worms, writhing, biting, and stinging Incessantly"—and he shuddered, as I did, at the revolting comparison.

> (Carpenter, 71)

Common in civilian and military populations, syphilis was a secret disease in bourgeois society because of its association with sexual promiscuity and immorality. It was rarely mentioned by name in fiction, though its symptoms might be described in detail, as above, whether to intrigue and to sermonize. Despite these taboos, it's been estimated that something like 10 percent of populations in urban centers had the disease (Carpenter). As Warren's "patient" attested, syphilis was a kind of animal within, transforming its victims into spectacles of pain and horror that might make them scarcely recognizable to themselves as human.

In scientific and medical circles, of course, syphilis was well known, commonly discussed and increasingly feared as a modern plague. Classified ads for cures—from the sarsaparilla root to the "balm of Syriacum"—filled the pages of Victorian periodicals, as did notices of doctors willing to treat the disease or offer scientific speculations on its causes and cures. Though the bacterium (*Treponema pallidum*) was not identified until the twentieth century, advances in knowledge about syphilis over the course of the nineteenth century were considerable. The notion that syphilis (the pox) was a stage of gonorrhea (the clap), for example, was disproved by the discovery that the latter had its own bacterial origins. Regardless of these medical details, there was a consensus that it was prostitutes who were responsible for the spread of the disease among soldiers, and both middle- and working-class men, who might then contaminate their wives, and thereby, threaten the moral and physical health of the entire nation. And because many such sexual encounters, especially those in the military, originated in Britain's far-flung imperial possessions, syphilis came to be viewed by the last quarter of the nineteenth century as a threat to the security of the Victorian empire as well (see **O is for Opium** and **D is for Dagga**).

Alarming reports from India filled the pages of *The Times* from the early 1860s onward, attributing the "nature of vice" to women camp followers who infected the soldiers, put them in hospital and cost the empire vast sums of money in lost manpower and medical costs. The mere proximity of the cantonments to Indian populations was also deemed a cause. Significantly, officials did not necessarily agree that venereal disease was more of a concern than, say, dysentery, typhus or cholera, which were also an enormous drain on military strength and medical resources (Levine, 41–42). But the moral anxiety around syphilis and related afflictions was extraordinarily powerful. Parliament passed Contagious Diseases Acts in 1864, 1866 and 1869 following a commission designed to investigate venereal diseases in Britain's armed forces. The Acts (whose very nomenclature protected Victorian eyes from the sight of venereal disease or syphilis) targeted prostitutes in specific port towns, authorizing their arrest, inspection and confinement in hospitals until they were cured. The CD Acts caused an uproar, not least from Victorian women reformers and feminists who were outraged by what they viewed as the instrumental rape through medical inspection of poor women and who were unafraid to speak out in public against such a violation of their bodily rights—even if such activism threw their own respectability into question. Josephine Butler spearheaded the cause, organizing for the repeal of the Acts through petitions and lobbying through her Ladies National Association for the Repeal of the Contagious Diseases Acts, a movement whose scale and effectiveness was virtually unprecedented.

The Acts were repealed in 1886, but the campaign continued, in large part because surveillance, regulation and medical inspection of prostitutes, both native and foreign, continued to flourish across the British Empire from India to Hong Kong to Fiji, Gibraltar and the Straits Settlements. Though this had been the case for decades, it was not until after repeal of the "domestic" legislation that Butler and the Ladies National Association (LNA) turned their attention to contagious diseases in India. Here, as at home, British women broke the Victorian taboo on speaking about venereal disease in general and syphilis in particular—a willingness aided by the fact that they did so on behalf of their poor suffering Indian "sisters." Butler's brand of Christian reform enthusiasm allowed her to defend Indian women against the interference of a colonizing state, but it did not necessarily mean she or her supporters viewed them as equals. The Repeal campaign at home and in the empire had class and race hierarchies built into it, so that "contagious disease" became a platform for promoting the cause of a decidedly Victorian imperial feminism: one in which white women intervened on behalf of brown women to save them from white men. While the health and welfare of Indian women was the ostensible rationale for the British women's repeal movement, Indian women were accorded very little agency. Indeed, the control of indigenous sexuality was arguably what was really at stake. The unchecked spread of diseases such as syphilis was a direct threat to both the viability of imperial rule and to claims about white superiority and invincibility (Levine, 2).

Repealers, for their part, openly admitted that venereal disease was a domestic concern: "It cannot be confined to the Army, but must permeate the whole of our social life... [and] cannot leave unimpaired the sanctity or happiness of the English home" (Burton, 157). Debates about Victorian syphilis, then, helped to shape a colonizing western feminist ethos, one with echoes down to the present. As well, the continuation of racialized forms of surveillance and bodily intervention from Delhi to Brisbane and beyond kept Victorian notions of sexual shame and legal repression alive down to the First World War, demonstrating how key the management of sexuality was as a strategy for gaining, and keeping, imperial power in the modern era.

Suggestions for Further Reading

Andrew, Elizabeth, and Katharine Bushnell. *The Queens Daughter's in India.* London: Morgan and Scott, 1899.

Burton, Antoinette. *Burdens of History: British Feminists, Indian Women and Imperial Culture, 1865–1915.* Chapel Hill: University of North Carolina Press, 1994.

Carpenter, Mary Wilson. *Health, Medicine and Society in Late Victorian England.* ABC-CLIO, 2010.

Levine, Philippa. *Prostitution, Race and Politics: Policing Venereal Disease in the British Empire.* London: Routledge, 2003.

Tambe, Ashwini. *Codes of Misconduct: Regulating Prostitution in Late Colonial Bombay.* Minneapolis: University of Minnesota Press, 2009.

S is also for ...

Santals
Sedition
Sekere, Nsuttahene Yaw
Sepoy
Singh, Ranjit

T is for Tatya Tope

CAPTURE OF TANTIA TOPEE. (See p. 283.)

Despite the concerted efforts of the British, the Indian rebel Tatya Tope remained elusive in the wake of the initial mutinies of 1857. This image shows his final capture. Print Collector.

It's a well-known fact that sepoys (from the Persian *sipahi*; Indian soldier in the East India Company army) mutinied against the British Empire in India in May 1857, and that after months and months of fighting, the rebellion was quelled. By August 1858, the Government of India Act had been passed, transferring control from the East India Company to the Crown in a re-organization of British rule in India designed to signal a new phase in the history of the Raj. By November 1858, Queen Victoria has issued her own proclamation, calling for all her Indian subjects to faithfully submit. Referring to recent mutinous events as "the acts of ambitious men," Victoria declared that "our power has been shown by the suppression of that rebellion in the field," and she expressed confidence in peace following the pardon of those who have been "misled, but who desire to return to the path of duty." Yet, the rebellion was not fully over until the spring of 1859— thanks in part to the determination of Tatya Tope, who threatened to retake the fallen cities of Kanpur and Lucknow, and kept the best and brightest of Britain's generals on the run in pursuit of him and his rebel sympathizers. Contrary to official pronouncements of the mutiny's suppression, and despite the Queen's confidence that the "leaders or instigators in revolt" had been summarily dealt with, Tope kept the unrest alive and well for the better part of a year after the Crown took over. He was a rebel leader who almost got away.

Tatya Tope's conflict with the British government of India was a far cry from the grievances of mutinous Indian soldiers, who rebelled for a combination of reasons related to the army's apparent indifference to their religious practices. The most famous of these is the incident of the greased cartridges, whereby sepoys rebelled against the practice of using ammunition greased with animal fat that was taboo. But there were other military challenges to dearly held native principles, such as the dispatch of sepoys to the conflicts in Burma, which involved crossing the *kala pani* (black waters, or ocean), considered a violation of caste. Tope's enmity stemmed from the long-standing association of his family with the court of Nana Saheb, a Maratha Brahmin who had been adopted by the last Peshwa of the Maratha Confederation. Born Ramachandra Pandurang Yewalekar in 1813 or 1814, Tope was a nickname: a reference to a bejeweled hat he was given and which is his signature in images of him from the period. Tatya Tope grew up in Peshwa's court, where his father was a supervisor in the official household. His childhood playmates were the young Nana Saheb and the Rani of Jhansi. Upon the Peshwa's death in 1851, the British refused to pay Nana Saheb his father's pension, using their prerogative to decide such matters and to determine which Indian rulers were fit to govern and which were not (known as the "doctrine of lapse"). That doctrine had eventuated in a series of takeovers of Indian states by the British in the 1850s, and Nana Saheb looked to be next. Despite sending an ambassador to Britain to make his case, Nana Saheb's hereditary right was denied, leaving him and his supporters, Tatya Tope included, feeling seriously aggrieved on the very eve of the mutiny (see **N is for Native Claim-making** and **K is for Kīngitanga**).

The circumstances under which Nana Saheb went from aggrieved ruler to sponsor of the rebellion have been a matter of debate in the century and a half since 1857. As the mutiny spread from Meerut to Delhi to Kanpur, the British looked to Nana Saheb to help them protect the garrison there as well as the treasury. But when the time came, he had been persuaded by rebel envoys to join the uprising, and in June 1857, he set about attacking the British entrenchment. Tatya Tope assumed the role of Nana Saheb's general, and under his leadership, British attempts to bring the subcontinent fully back under their control stretched from days and months into the better part of two years.

By all contemporary accounts, Tatya Tope was an extremely effectively leader of a rebel army said to be 20,000-strong. He gave experienced generals such as Wheeler and Havelock a run for their money, not just at Kanpur, but also in battles at Gwalior, Kalpi and into the forests of Rajasthan. Though his successes were temporary— the British eventually took back Kanpur and Gwalior—his capacity to raise fresh troops after each setback and his ability to elude capture was impressive. One observer called him "the swift-footed guerilla chief," while *The Times* remarked on his knack for the chase: "Tatya Tope seems to be ubiquitous. With half a dozen columns after him, he manages to slip through them. Several native chiefs are friendly to Tatya, which makes his arrest and chase difficult." *The Times* marveled equally at his skill at evading capture: "Everybody in authority pretends to know where Tatya was yesterday, notwithstanding that he turns up tomorrow in very different and distant quarters, which he could hardly have marched in that interval." He was compared to "a duck in a lake who suddenly dives and comes up where least expected" (Dharaiya, 110). General Sylvester, his opponent on the field no less, called him "the genius of flight."

Yet, in the end, he was captured. The British were especially determined to bring in Tatya and Nana Saheb because of their association with the massacre of the boats during the siege of Kanpur. Nana Sahib had promised British residents—among them women and children—safe passage to Allahabad. But as they were loaded into boats to cross the Ganges, they were fired on from the shore by sepoys who supported the uprising, and in the melee that followed, most of the men were killed, and the women and children who survived were seconded to the infamous Bibighar (House of Ladies) where they too were eventually massacred. The British held Nana Saheb and his commander-in-chief, Tatya Tope, responsible for the boat scene, though in his court-martial deposition, Tope denied the charge. He was nonetheless hanged in April 1859. Interestingly, his legendary escape talents live on. As late as the 1970s, scholars in India debated whether the man whom the British had caught was actually Tope—or a substitute planted to allow him to elude capture. In the long historical memory of 1857, then, he remains a figure of mythic proportions, a rebel who may have or may not have cheated death, but who nonetheless made putting an end to the mutiny an especially strenuous task for the guardians of the Raj.

Suggestions for Further Reading

Bates, Crispin, and Marina Carter, eds. *Mutiny at the Margins: New Perspectives on the Indian Uprising of 1857,* Volume III: *Global Perspectives.* New Delhi: SAGE Publications, 2013.

Chakraborty, Kaushik. *Decolonising the Revolt of 1857.* Kolkata: Reader's Service, 2007.

Dharaiya, R. K. *Gujarat in 1857.* Ahmedabad: Gujarat University, 1970.

Edwards, Michael. *Red Year: The Indian Rebellion of 1857.* London: Hamilton, 1973.

Joshi, P. C. *1857 in Folk Songs.* New Delhi: People's Publishing House, 1994.

Nayar, Pramod. *The Penguin 1857 Reader.* Delhi: Penguin, 2007.

Sharpe, Jenny. *Allegories of Empire: The Figure of Woman in the Colonial Text.* Minneapolis: University of Minnesota Press, 1993.

T is also for . . .

Te Kooti
Telegraph
Terrorism
Tewfik, Khedive of Egypt
Trinidad Muhurram

U

is for Urabi

This image of Urabi and his troops riding through Alexandria in 1882 is from The Graphic, which covered the uprising and allowed Victorian readers to see in vivid terms what the forces of dissent and disruption looked like in Egypt. Illustration by S. Durand, The Graphic, July 22, 1882, Hulton Archive.

On the eve of the British bombardment of Alexandria in July 1882, Colonel Ahmed Urabi wrote a letter to *The Times* of London addressed to Prime Minister William Ewart Gladstone, telling him that there was still time to come to terms with Egypt rather than to begin a war. It read in part:

Our Prophet in his Koran has commanded us not to seek war nor to begin it. He had commanded us also, if war be waged against us, to resist, and under penalty of being ourselves as unbelievers, to follow those who have assailed us with every weapon and without pity.

Hence England may rest assured that the first gun she fires on Egypt will absolve the Egyptians from all treaties, contracts, and conventions, that the control and debt will cease, that the property of Europeans will be confiscated, that the canals will be destroyed, the communications cut.

And that use will be made of the religious zeal of Mahommedans to preach a holy war in Syria, Arabia and in India.... England, in fine, may rest assured that we are determined to fight, to die martyrs for our country—as has been enjoined on us by our Prophet—or else to conquer and so live independently and happy. Happiness in either case is promised to us, and when a people is imbued with this belief their courage knows no bounds. (Harlow and Carter, 147)

The letter did not reach Gladstone in time and it went unanswered. The invasion of Egypt proceeded, and Urabi was defeated in the battle of Tel-el-Kabir in the fall of 1882; he was tried and sentenced first to death and then to banishment for life. He lived in Ceylon (Sri Lanka) until the turn of the twentieth century; he then returned to Egypt and died there in 1911.

Urabi's revolution was short-lived, but it stemmed from deep frustrations with colonial rule. Not withstanding its failure, by the mid-twentieth century, it had earned him credit for being one of the founders of modern Egyptian nationalism (see **K is for Kīngitanga**; **N is for Native Claim-making**; and **J is for Jihad**). Historians have argued over the causes of the revolt. Some see state failure in the tumultuous challenge to the imperial status quo; others, an experiment in free trade gone badly wrong; still others, the power of a multi-class reform movement to upend conventional notions imperial hegemony (Cole). In fact, the revolt that Urabi led stemmed from long-simmering resentments about the crushing debt to which Egypt was subject and about the ways that Europeans—British and French—profited from both that stranglehold and the advantages, if not monopoly, that had on the military and the civil service. The rise of a vibrant print culture in this period, combined with an increasingly literate public eager for political journalism that articulated its grievances and imagined redress was also key to the appeal of Urabi. Urabi was, for his part, what the Egyptians call an *ibn al-balad* ("son of the country") who had a modern education and the experience of military service. His upstart biography gave him popular appeal as a critic of the Khedive—technically a vassal of the Ottoman Empire, but commonly viewed as the puppet of European interests. In the wake of the formation of the Egyptian National Party in 1879, Urabi threw himself and the army behind the reformers; supported by the peasants, the revolutionaries aimed to oust foreign rule from both Egypt and the Sudan. Amid calls for a constitutional platform and a national congress, Egyptians took to the streets in Alexandria, in part, because "a generalized hostility to Europeans could easily become a hatred for the Egyptian state itself" (Cole, 211).

Urabi's defeat was a blow to anything like aspirations to parliamentary democracy in Egypt. The British occupation, intended to be brief, continued until 1956. Back in Britain, a campaign to save Urabi from execution was afoot, led by Wilfred Scawen Blunt, an English poet and writer who had been a member of the Diplomatic Service and was an ardent supporter of several nineteenth-century nationalist causes. He wrote letters to the *The Times*, called on politicians to alert them to Urabi's plight and created a legal defense fund to which he himself contributed significant money. His criticisms of the British occupation and his support for Urabi caused him to be banned from Egypt for four years, and the links he made between Irish and Egyptian nationalism made him no friend to the imperial establishment whether in London or Cairo. His 1912 book on the Irish struggle was entitled *The Land War in Ireland, Being a Personal Narrative of Events, in Continuation of "A Secret History of the English Occupation of Egypt"* and made an energetic case for critiques of Gladstone's Egyptian and Irish polices and for sympathies between "the Catholic and the Mohammedan" (2, 6). He drew his friend and fellow writer Lady Gregory, the Irish nationalist and revivalist, into his Urabi campaign. She, too, wrote a letter to *The Times* in October 1882 called "Arabi and His Household," which painted an affective picture of the rebel as a *pater familias* that caused quite a sensation in establishment circles; even Gladstone was said to admire her efforts (DiBattista and McDiarmid, 218–219).

Blunt and Gregory were anti-imperialists who "tumbled into a revolution" (DiBattista and McDiarmid, 218). Urabi's revolution was itself, in turn, the result of a challenge by Urabi and his fellow officers that precipitated a confrontation with the khedive with largely unanticipated results. Their political struggle might be seen as anti-imperial in a confessional idiom: In his letter to Gladstone, Urabi invoked the idea of holy war, or jihad (see **J is for Jihad**). The revolt he spearheaded is too complex to be reduced to that, and the credit Urabi gets should be tempered by recognition of the power of class struggles and an equal variety of actors, including the peasants whose rejection of usurious European debt was key to galvanizing support for the revolution. Meanwhile, the war over Egypt waged in the pages of *The Times* is a reminder of how often, and with what great stakes, evidence of empire made it to the sightline of Victorian readers, the majority of whom likely had little direct connection to a place such as Egypt, but who witnessed its unfolding, and from time to time, its unraveling, before their eyes (see **B is for Bold Fenian Men** and **J is for Jihad**).

Suggestions for Further Reading

Blunt, Wilfred Scawen. *Secret History of the English Occupation of Egypt*. New York: Knopf, 1907.

Cole, Juan R. *Colonialism and Revolution in the Middle East: Social and Cultural Origins of Egypt's 'Urabi Movement*. Princeton: Princeton University Press, 1993.

DiBattista, Maria, and Lucy McDiarmid, eds. *High and Low Moderns: Literature and Culture, 1889–1939*. Oxford: Oxford University Press, 1996.

Esmeir, Samera, *Juridical Humanity: A Colonial History*. Palo Alto: Stanford University Press, 2014.

Harlow, Barbara, and Marina Carter, eds. *Imperialism and Orientalism*. Oxford: Blackwell, 1999.

Reid, Donald Malcolm. "The 'Urabi Revolution and the British Conquest, 1879–1882" in Martin W. Daly and Carl F. Petry, eds, *The Cambridge History of Egypt*. Cambridge: Cambridge University Press, 1998, v. 2.

U is also for . . .

Uitlanders
Ulster
Ulundi, battle of
Universal suffrage
Unions

 is for "Vande Mataram"

"Vande Mataram," the hymn to Mother India, was inspired by images of Indian women of all kinds. In this tableau, exhibited in aid of women's medical missions to India, the death of Savitri is depicted.

Mother, I salute thee!
Rich with thy hurrying streams,
bright with orchard gleams,
Cool with thy winds of delight,
Dark fields waving Mother of might,
Mother free.

Glory of moonlight dreams,
Over thy branches and lordly streams,
Clad in thy blossoming trees,
Mother, giver of ease
Laughing low and sweet!
Mother I kiss thy feet,
Speaker sweet and low!
Mother, to thee I salute.

Who hath said thou art weak in thy lands
When the swords flash out in seventy million hands
And seventy million voices roar
Thy dreadful name from shore to shore?
With many strengths who art mighty and stored,
To thee I call Mother and Lord!
Though who savest, arise and save!
To her I cry who ever her foeman drove
Back from plain and Sea

And shook herself free.
Thou art wisdom, thou art law,
Thou art heart, our soul, our breath
Though art love divine, the awe
In our hearts that conquers death.
Thine the strength that nerves the arm,
Thine the beauty, thine the charm.
Every image made divine
In our temples is but thine.

Thou art Durga, Lady and Queen,
With her hands that strike and her

swords of sheen,
Thou art Lakshmi lotus-throned,
And the Muse a hundred-toned,
Pure and perfect without peer,
Mother lend thine ear,
Rich with thy hurrying streams,
Bright with thy orchard gleems,
Dark of hue O candid-fair

In thy soul, with bejeweled hair
And thy glorious smile divine,
Loveliest of all earthly lands,
Showering wealth from well-stored hands!
Mother, mother mine!
Mother sweet, I salute thee,
Mother great and free!

In the quiet solitude of his study, sometime in the early 1870s, the Bengali poet and novelist Bankim Chandra Chatterjee penned the above verses, imagining Mother India as the avatar of the not-yet nation. The original poem, written in a mixture of Bangla and Sanskrit, remained unpublished for nearly a decade until it appeared as a text in his 1882 novel *Anandamath*. By the time the novel was published, Chatterjee was an established author and literary editor; in fact, like many Victorian novels, this one was serialized in the Bengali *Bangadarshan*, which Chatterjee had founded in 1872. Though *Anandamath* has been lauded as one of the most significant Bengali novels of the nineteenth century and as one of the literary bases of Bengali nationalism, one of its most enduring legacies is "Vande Mataram" itself. Translated into both English and numerous vernaculars, and widely considered to be the anthem of Indian independence, this short poem became a vehicle for anti-British sentiment and a lightning rod for communal politics down to the present.

Anandamath is based on the story of the Sannyasi, Hindu ascetics who staged a rebellion against the British in the 1770s in the middle of a raging famine in Bengal. Critics then and now have read the novel as a call for a Hindu-inspired nationalist movement to rise up and drive the British out of India. The book was banned not simply for its all-India appeal, but also because it was an inspiration for early twentieth-century Bengali terrorists who were said to carry it with them, along with copies of the *Bhagavad Gita*, as they undertook their anarchic work to bring down the Raj. Bankim did not intend to write a strictly historical novel; the plot is more like a political myth suited to the sentiments of Victorian Bengal, where a romantic plot about Hindus organizing "against the oppressors to bring back the pristine glory of the motherland" (Mukherjee) had appeal among the *bhadralok.* "Vande Mataram" was key to that storyline: recited at various key moments of battle or self-recognition on the part of the protagonist, one Mahendra, who aspires to be a *santan* (progeny; disciple). Despite the centrality of mother-love to the ode, *santan* status required renunciation of all worldly goods and relationships and the embrace of an ascetic masculine warrior culture where women worked in service to the householder. In the words of an exemplary rebel, "the Motherland is our only mother. Our Motherland is higher than heaven. Mother India is our mother. We have no other mother. We have no father, no brother, no sister, no wife, no children, no home, no hearth—all we have is the Mother."

As the embodiment of these claims, "Vande Mataram" gained iconic status in Indian nationalist politics within a decade of its appearance in *Anandamath* (see **N is for Native Claim-making**). Set to music by Rabindranath Tagore, it was sung at the annual meeting of the Indian National Congress in 1896 and it became a popular rallying cry in swadeshi demonstrations during the struggles around the partition of Bengal. In the context of empire, allegories of the kind that "Vande Mataram" conjured were considered threatening to state security: By 1910, the novel was on the Proscribed Publications list and the *Encyclopedia Britannica* was warning against the "dangerous meanings in the mouths of unscrupulous agitators" that the singing of the song provoked. Nor did the controversy end there. Because of the popular momentum it gained as a nationalist song, "Vande Mataram" was considered by some to be the official song of India. Before 1947, a number of Indian Muslim nationalists objected to the Hindu-inflected character of the tune, labeling it idolatry, and as such, inimical to a truly inclusive subcontinental nationalism. These debates carried on into the 1930s when Congress convened a special committee on the issue. As recently as the early twenty-first century, there have been insinuations that "Vande Mataram" was an early species of Hindutva: a rallying cry for Hindu fundamentalism by any other name. From its Victorian literary roots comes a powerful delivery system for all kinds of struggle over how postcolonial India can—and should—represent itself.

Suggestions for Further Reading

Bhattacharya, Sabyasachi. *Vande Mataram: The Biography of a Song.* Delhi: Penguin Books India, 2003.

Chatterji, Bankimchandra. *Anandamath, or The Sacred Brotherhood.* Oxford: Oxford University Press, 2005.

Mukherjee, Menakshi. *The Perishable Empire: Essays on Indian Writing in English.* Delhi: Oxford India, 2003.

Singhal, V. K. *Patriots and Ballads at Gallows: Vande Mataram Saga.* Delhi: Kalpaz Publications, 2007.

Sinha, Mrinalini. *Specters of Mother India: The Global Restructuring of an Empire.* Durham: Duke University Press, 2006.

Tagore, Rabindranath. *The Writings of Rabindranath Tagore: A Miscellany.* Calcutta: Sahitya Akademi, 1994.

V is also for . . .

Vale of Peshawar
Vellore Mutiny
Vereeniging, Treaty of
Victoria, Empress of India
Voortrekker

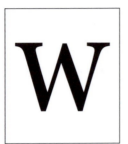

W is for Winston Churchill

Winston Churchill was the veteran of several Victorian imperial campaigns. He is pictured at the threshold of his tent in 1900 in South Africa, where he was a war correspondent in the Anglo-Boer War. Universal Images Group.

Like Mohandas Gandhi, Winston Churchill is typically thought of as a twentieth-century figure, but he was, in fact, in many ways very much a Victorian—a very late Victorian, perhaps, but a Victorian nonetheless (see **G is for Gandhi**). He admitted as much in his 1930 autobiography *My Early Life*, which chronicled his story from his childhood to his marriage less than ten years into the new twentieth century. Churchill believed that the end of the Victorian century came with the death in 1903 of Lord Salisbury, who had been secretary of state for India, Foreign Secretary and Prime Minister (twice). "The world in which Lord Salisbury had reigned ...[was] soon to be separated from us by gulfs and chasms such as have rarely opened in so brief a space. Little could we foresee ... the awful convulsions which would shake the world and shiver into fragments the structures of the nineteenth century," Churchill wrote. "The new century of storm and change had already embraced the British Empire in its fierce grip" (370).

Born in 1874, just five years after Gandhi, Churchill had lived much of the fin de siècle in the grip of imperial war. His mother was an American and his father, an English aristocrat. His earliest memory was a military one: His grandfather, the Duke of Marlborough, had been appointed Lord Lieutenant of Ireland, and Churchill recalled being impressed by a ceremony in Dublin during which the Duke unveiled a statue of Lord Gough, hero of the Peninsular Wars, the Mahratta Wars and the first Opium War (see **O is for Opium**). A graduate of Harrow, Churchill struggled to pass the entrance examination for Sandhurst, but was eventually "gazetted" to the 4th Hussars. Not perhaps a natural soldier, he made his way to Victorian battlefronts as either a war correspondent or as a chronicler of colonial campaigns. The first of these was Cuba, which despite the fact that he arrived in the middle of a long, drawn-out guerilla campaign, he approached with an adventurism that he himself likened to the spirit of boyish excitement of Robert Louis Stevenson's *Treasure Island*. He wrote about the Spanish War for the *Daily Graphic*, the first of several such commissions. From there, he went to India, where he mostly played polo and encountered Edward Gibbon's *History of the Decline and Fall of the Roman Empire*, which had been published in that anticolonial revolutionary year of 1776. "Quite a big place, India!" he remarked, logging accounts of his travel, his polo playing and the doggerel he had heard in the sergeants' mess, including this tuneful homage to Queen Victoria, Empress of India:

> Great White Mother, far across the sea,
> Ruler of the Empire may she ever be.
> Long may she reign, glorious and free
> In the Great White Motherland. (125)

But it was not until he went to the Northwest Frontier in 1897 to observe the British try to contain a series of Pashtun uprisings that Churchill began to make his name as a reporter (see **A is for the Afghan Wars**). He captured the mud and sweat of the battle in dispatches for *The Telegraph* and *The Pioneer*, and joined the battle himself, under the command of General Jeffrey of the Malakand Field Force. From the perspective of his 1930 memoir, he viewed the tribal natives as "pestilential," though his accounts written closer in time to the campaign are filled with far more orientalist and pathologizing views of the enemies, whose murderous blood pacts and "savage" attacks he roundly condemned, but not before admitting that they had their effects. The British were on the defensive throughout the campaign: "Like men in a leaking ship, who toil at the pumps ceaselessly and find their fatigues increasing and the ship sinking hour by hour, they cast anxious weary eyes in the direction whence help might be expected. But none came." They wearied under the repetitive cut and thrust, advance and retreat; they found it hard to claim decisive victories; and in the end, they fire-bombed the villages they could not otherwise subdue. They took a drubbing in the press, where Churchill's desperate accounts ratified fears that Afghanistan and environs could not be settled—again (see **A is for the Afghan Wars**). And Churchill got a close-up look at jihad, as the mad fakir of Swat, Saidullah, whipped up anti-British fighters and evaded capture (see **J is for Jihad**).

His book on the subject, *The Story of the Malakand Field Force*, secured Churchill's reputation as witness to the challenges of—and to—British hegemony on the ground. It also got him the attention of Lord Salisbury, whom Churchill viewed as "the Great Man" and "Master of the British World" (163). Churchill followed shortly thereafter with *The River War*, his account of the Mahdist revolt in the Sudan. Though, like many Victorian soldiers, he was ever eager for the next battle scene (as he wrote, "I was deeply anxious to share in this"), his desire to be in the mix did not necessarily sit well with the War Office (161). But he managed to obtain permission to accompany the 21st Lancers, and to write dispatches for the *Morning Post*, and he soon found himself at the battle of Omdurman. Whether dilating on the thrill of battle or on the virulence of the Muslim enemy, he could scarcely contain himself. Of "Mahommedans" he wrote, "Besides the fanatical frenzy, which is as dangerous in a man as hydrophobia in a dog, there is this fearful fatalistic apathy ... no stronger retrograde force exists in the world." Yet, he conceded that Islam was hardly moribund; it was energetic and dynamic and a genuine threat to British imperialism. In both his memoirs and *The River War*, he left eyewitness accounts of one of the most decisive battles in the scramble for Africa. Equipped with a Mauser automatic pistol, he made his own small contribution to the cause by felling several foes astride a horse and brandishing gleaming curved swords (191). After the worst of the battle was over, he donated some skin from his forearm as a graft to aid the wound of a friend. Churchill considered the scar a souvenir of a job well done.

A serial campaigner, Churchill's final war of the nineteenth century was in South Africa, where he was commissioned as a reporter and a soldier both and spent time as a prisoner of war during the Anglo-Boer War. If these Victorian experiences of battle held any lesson for the great statesman of the twentieth century, it was that war was, in his view, akin to "ordinary life": if you are well prepared, and especially well armed, "lots of enemies will give you wide berth" (192). How in character he was to mourn Salisbury's passing, and with it, the coming of a century "of fearful wars and terrors unmeasured and renewing" (370) that would dwarf even Victoria's imperial wars considerably.

Suggestions for Further Reading

Churchill, Winston. *My Early Life, 1874–1904*. New York: Charles Scribner's, 1930.
Churchill, Winston. *The River War: An Historical Account of the Reconquest of the Soudan*. London: Longman's, 1902.
Coughlin, Con. *Churchill's First War: Young Winston at War with the Afghans*. London: St. Martin's Press, 2014.
Herman, Arthur. *Gandhi & Churchill: The Epic Rivalry that Destroyed an Empire and Forged Our Age*. New York: Bantam, 2009.
Toye, Richard. *Churchill's Empire: The World that Made Him and the World He Made*. London: Henry Holt, 2010.

W is also for . . .

Wahhabism
Waitangi, Treaty of
War of Water
White Australia Policy
Wolesely, Sir Garnet

X is for Xhosaland

Long after the end of the mid-nineteenth-century cattle killings, the amaXhosa live on in memory, as this memorial to the "victims" illustrates. The local heroine of the events, Nongqawuse, has also had many afterlives in various forms of cultural production, serving as a touchstone for global anti-apartheid imaginaries to this day. Photo taken in March 2008 and provided with permission, courtesy of Andrew Offenburger.

On February 18, 1857, the sun rose as usual over the lands of the
amaXhosa people in southern Africa. This everyday occurrence was a
source of particular disappointment and distress for the amaXhosa,
however, as Nongqawuse, a teenaged prophetess, had promised that
the sun would rise red in the sky and the spirits of deceased amaXhosa
ancestors would return to expel white settlers from their lands.
Nongqawuse had claimed that the ancestors demanded the Xhosa kill
all their cattle (a source of both food and wealth) and destroy all their
crops in order to bring about this spiritual undertaking. Those who
had followed the instructions of Nongqawuse and the ancestors
and dutifully destroyed all sources of food soon found themselves
starving and at the mercy of British colonial administrators, who, as
in Ireland, sought to use famine to achieve their own geopolitical
objectives. The Great Cattle Killing of 1856–1857, as it was soon
known, initiated both a disastrous period in the history of the
amaXhosa people and a pivotal turning point in the history of British
colonization in southern Africa (see **N is for Native Claim-making**
and **K is for Kīngitanga**).

The amaXhosa are a Bantu-speaking people who had come to
inhabit the lands in southern Africa generally east of the Great Fish
River and along the coast in the modern South African provinces of
Eastern Cape and KwaZulu-Natal. The amaXhosa had a lengthy
history of trade and contact with the Khoikhoi and San peoples of
Southern Africa; all groups soon found themselves in conflict with
the new Dutch-speaking colonists of the Cape after the latter's arrival
in the late seventeenth century. The expansion of Dutch-descended
Trekboers beyond the initial settlements of Cape Town in search of
fertile farmland led to eventual conflict with the amaXhosa. The
Trekboers and the amaXhosa competed over farmland, grazing areas
and cattle themselves, resulting in three frontier wars between 1778
and 1803. These wars were largely inconclusive, and the amaXhosa

were able to maintain much of their territory in spite of Boer attempts at encroachment.

Circumstances changed, however, following the permanent annexation of the Cape Colony by the British government in 1806, in the midst of the Napoleonic Wars. At this point the British colonial administration became concerned with the issue of rapidly expanding Boer settlers and constant conflict with the amaXhosa. British colonial administrators sought to deal with colonial skirmishes by moving more troops along with the settlers, which the amaXhosa interpreted as an invasion of their lands and sovereignty, resulting in two further frontier wars in 1811–1812 and 1818–1819. To counter the very present threat of amaXhosa invasions, the British government approved an emigration scheme in 1820 of 4,000 British settlers to the region, in an attempt to shore up the porous nature of the frontier with an area of dense settlement. Additional movements of troops and the planting of forts along the frontier supplemented these acts of purposeful settler occupation.

These moves at settlement were often accompanied by treaties that insisted on expulsion of amaXhosa polities from areas increasingly settled by Europeans, and the subsequent creation of a "neutral" area where both European and amaXhosa settlement was forbidden (in each instance, these prohibitions were soon ignored). Continued European settler expansion into Xhosaland led to piecemeal British attempts to claim territory at the expense of the amaXhosa polities, and soon led again to a sixth frontier war from 1834 to 1835. The amaXhosa were led, in part, by the able chieftain Hintsa ka Khawuta, who was a member of the Gcaleka subgroup of the amaXhosa. Following this war and a subsequent frontier war in the 1840s, the British increasingly claimed territory from the amaXhosa. By the early 1850s, Xhosaland was increasingly squeezed between an expanding Cape Colony and the new British colony of Natal (annexed from Boers who had, in turn, claimed much of the land from the amaZulu; see **R is for Riel, Louis**).

By the early 1850s, the constant movement of settlers into African territory had resulted in the increased commitment of British colonial officials to military defense of this expansion. The amaXhosa continued to significantly challenge this invasion, however, offering significant resistance, and creating a frontier that was only haphazardly occupied. Two arrivals in the mid-1850s would significantly change the situation between the British and the amaXhosa in Xhosaland: Governor George Grey and lung-sickness disease. Prior to taking his post in the Cape, Grey had served as governor in South Australia and New Zealand (and would return to New Zealand for most of his life after his time in southern Africa). His time in both colonies had led him to take a paternalistic view of indigenous peoples that saw them as obstacles to larger imperial aims; this was no exception in the Cape. The continued pressing of British settlers and soldiers on the amaXhosa was only compounded by the sudden occurrence of lung sickness among Xhosa cattle. Scores of cattle died, depriving the amaXhosa both of a source of food and social currency, and leading to further disruption. It was at this moment in 1856 that the teenaged Nongqawuse first saw her vision of the ancestors, promising her not only the driving of the rapacious Europeans from Xhosaland, but the revitalization of health and strength of the amaXhosa people. Word of her vision spread. When prominent chief Sarhili ka Hintsa began slaughtering his cattle and burning his crops, others soon followed suit. The Great Cattle Killing had begun.

The failure of the promised red sun spelled disaster for amaXhosa resistance to British imperial aims, and George Grey pressed his advantage as much as he could. Hundreds of thousands of cattle were killed, and tens of thousands of amaXhosa starved to death. Grey forbade European assistance to the starving amaXhosa unless they, in turn, entered into labor contracts with British farmers and surrendered independent tribal existences in disputed areas. Thus, Grey used the famine in order to enact larger imperial policies over the area and to attack indigenous resistance (see **F is for Famine**). Most of the remaining Xhosaland was annexed as British Kaffraria to the Cape Colony by 1866, and following a final frontier war in 1878, amaXhosa autonomy was largely eliminated in the face of imperial expansion.

The tragedy of the Great Cattle Killing has been hotly debated by historians. Today, it is largely seen as one of many millenarian movements that occurred in the nineteenth century in the face of incredible social disruption and violence. The violence of decades of imperial expansion and the devastation of the cattle lung sickness worked to create the right conditions for this millenarian movement. The failure of the red sun's rise offered more than a frustration of millenarian hopes. The cattle killings (which have been powerfully memorialized—see the accompanying image from 2008) also offered an opportunity for imperial manipulation of disaster and the potential for ending a century of indigenous African resistance to colonization.

Note: Thousands of indigenous languages were spoken across Victoria's empire, and their persistence represented one vector of stubborn resistance to the British. IsiXhosa, the language spoken by the Xhosa people of eastern coastal areas of what is now South Africa, has an orthography studded with letters that represent sounds that do not exist in English. *Xh*, for example, represents the sound that Westerners use to encourage a horse to giddyap—a sliding, slurpy click sound produced on the side of the mouth as the tongue pulls away from the inside edges of one's top teeth. *Q*, as in the name Nonquawuse, is a rounded and resonant sound produced when confidently pulling the tip of the tongue away from the top of the mouth.

Suggestions for Further Reading

Bradford, Helen. "Women, Gender and Colonialism: Rethinking the History of the British Cape Colony and Its Frontier Zones, c. 1806–70," *Journal of African History* 37 (1996).

Crais, Clifton. *White Supremacy and Black Resistance in Pre-industrial South Africa: The Making of the Colonial Order in the Eastern Cape, 1770–1865.* Cambridge: Cambridge University Press, 1992.

Mda, Zakes. *The Heart of Redness: A Novel.* New York: Picador, 2000.

Mostert, Neil. *Frontiers: The Epic of South Africa's Creation and the Tragedy of the Xhosa People.* New York: Knopf, 1992.

Peires, Jeff. *The Dead Will Arise: Nongqawuse and the Great Xhosa Cattle-Killing Movement of 1856–7.* Bloomington: Indiana University Press, 1989.

Stapleton, Timothy J. "'They No Longer Care for Their Chiefs': Another Look at the Xhosa Cattle-Killing of 1856–1857," *The International Journal of African Historical Studies* 24, 2 (1991): 383–392.

Wenzel, Jennifer. *Bulletproof: Afterlives of Anticolonial Prophecy in South Africa and Beyond.* Chicago: University of Chicago Press, 2009.

X is also for . . .

Y is for Yakub Khan

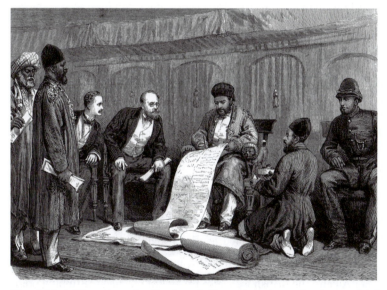

Here, Yakub Khan signs the Gandamak Treaty in 1879 under the watchful eye of the British agent, Major Louis Cavagnari. The treaty was to prove fateful for them both. Cavagnari was assassinated shortly thereafter, and Yakub Khan was considered a traitor by Afghans for negotiating. He abdicated and was exiled by the British after the Second Anglo-Afghan War that ensued. Universal Images Group.

Yakub Khan (b. 1849–d. 1923) might hold the record as the briefest-reigning amir in modern Afghan history. Inheriting the throne upon the death of his father Sher Ali on February 21, 1879, he ruled until October 12, less than eight months. From the British imperial perspective, Yakub's historical importance lay in his role in "the Cabul Mutiny" of 1879, when Afghan troops and city inhabitants stormed the British Residency in Kabul, killing the envoy, Sir Louis Cavagnari, and his guards. British commentators at the time, and well into the future, debated whether Yakub encouraged the rebellion or simply refused to stop it. Either way, Yakub was viewed as central to one of the most infamous moments of insurrection and chaos in the British Empire.

The Afghan siege of the British Residency can be traced to newly rising tensions between old enemies, Russia and Britain. Britain, ever anxious over its possession of India, figured Afghanistan as a border country that needed to be controlled, if not settled (see **A is for the Afghan Wars**). Sher Ali, who began his rule as amir in 1869, negotiated with the British on the condition that they not station an officer in Kabul. He reasoned that the Afghan population, famously heterogeneous in tribe and ethnicity, were in fact united over the fear of losing sovereignty to a European power, a possibility that would be signaled by such a presence. At home, things were a mess. In 1873, Sher Ali declared a younger son, and not Yakub, to be his successor. Yakub and his brother Ayub rebelled, leading the amir to imprison Yakub and exile Ayub to Persia. Over the next few years, the relations between Sher Ali and the British were also rocky, but reached the tipping point when the British learned that a Russian mission had forced its way into Kabul in 1878. Lord Lytton had taken over as viceroy, and eager to carry out the hawkish "forward policy" of the current British government led by Benjamin Disraeli, delivered an ultimatum to Sher Ali to accept a British envoy. Not giving him enough time to respond, the British declared war and invaded, initiating the Second Anglo-Afghan War (1879–1881). Sher Ali sought support from the Russians, but was coldly refused. He died in Mazar-i-Sharif soon after, leaving the throne to Yakub, whom he had recently released from prison.

Yakub thus became ruler of Afghanistan under less than auspicious circumstances. Finding himself at the helm of an invaded country, and with no Russian support in sight, he signed the Treaty of Gandamak with the British in May 1879. Negotiated by Cavagnari, the treaty stipulated that the British return Kandahar and Jellalabad to Yakub, afford him and his successors a handsome subsidy, and support him militarily if attacked. In return, Yakub gave the British contested territories, including Pishin, Sibi, Kurram and the Khyber Pass as well as control of Afghan foreign policy; agreed to a free trade relation with India; and, portentously, allowed them to install a permanent mission in Kabul. Lytton and Disraeli rejoiced. However, in September, unarmed Afghan troops arrived at Bala Hissar, the ancient fortress where Yakub held court, demanding to receive back pay for months of uncompensated service. Turned away, they went to the British mission, where guards shot at them. The Afghan troops retreated only to return with weapons and Kabuli residents, and besieged the mission, killing Cavagnari and his guards. British troops, led by General Frederick Roberts, arrived in Logar Valley, where Yakub met them and abdicated, reportedly telling Roberts that he "would rather be a grass-cutter in the British camp than ruler of Afghanistan" ("Ex-Ammer's Death"). The British exiled Yakub to India, and General Roberts proceeded to decimate Kabul in retaliation.

While Yakub was clearly a part of the disorder, dissent and disruption with which the British had to reckon as they strove to manage Afghanistan, by most British accounts, he was neither heroic nor inspiring. For example, G. A. Henty's adventure novel for boys, *For Name or Fame, or through Afghan Passes* (1886), features an Afghan character, the young boy Youssouf, who refers to Yakub as "weak" and "no better than a reed to lean upon" (203). Recent Anglo-American historians similarly cast Yakub as ineffectual. Edgar O'Ballance refers to Yakub as "something of a compromise candidate" at the time of his ascension (41), while Ewans describes him as "a broken reed" (96). From the Afghan perspective, one could look at the self-congratulatory memoir of his successor, Abdur Rahman, who ruled from 1880 until his death in 1901. Arguing for the relative stability of his regime, Abdur Rahman takes Yakub and his brother to task for rebelling against their father: "The people had got into such bad habits of living and mischief, that as the eldest sons of the then Amir, Shere Ali, named Yakub and Ayub, revolted against their own father at Herat, one may consider that if the sons of the King set such a good, virtuous example, what lessons might not the subjects have learned from them!" (228). It is especially Yakub's signing of the Gandamak Treaty that seems to condemn him from an Afghan perspective. Historian Louis Dupree, writing in 1980, declared that present-day Afghans still think of it as "the most disgraceful agreement ever signed by an amir" and that they refer to it as "'the Condemned Treaty'" (409, 425).

But are there different ways to tell this story? At times, historians seem to express sympathy for Yakub, passed over and imprisoned by his father, forced into signing the Gandamak Treaty, and hamstrung by history. Even the anonymous author of *Blackwood's* "The Ex-Amir Yakub Khan: From the Note-Book of a Staff Officer" (1880), who is singularly devoted to proving the Amir's complicity in the uprising, notes that Yakub's signing of the treaty, "place[d] him in the predicament of a man with one leg in one boat, and the other in another" (762). When the Afghan troops and city dwellers attacked the British mission, the author writes, Yakub must have thought it better not to interfere and that, "if once he were to order his guns to open on men who were clearing his country of infidels, it would be hopeless for him any longer to think of ruling Afghanistan" ("The Ex-Amir Yakub Khan," 762). Remarkable for its creative, although Orientalizing, inhabiting of an Afghan perspective, the sentence suggests how Yakub occupied a lose-lose situation. It also asks us to think about how the assigning of moral values or personal flaws like "weakness" to political figures personalizes much larger forces. Calling a leader "weak" deflects attention from the machinations of imperial ideology (for instance, the anonymous author's characterization of the Afghan attackers as "swarms of bees" with no definite purpose, rather than, say, the other side of the binary, patriotic defenders of their homeland) ("The Ex-Amir Yakub Khan," 759). It also seems implicitly to lay the responsibility for deaths, both Afghan and British, on the shoulders of the imperialized, justifying the British imposition of a "strong" leader in Kabul. However others judge him, we can view the controversy surrounding Yakub, with his rapid ascension and abdication and his questionable role in the Kabul uprising of 1879, as signaling the unquellable unrest and discord that met the British as they attempted to control Afghanistan.

Suggestions for Further Reading

'Abd al-Raḥmān Khān (Amir of Afghanistan). *The Life of Amir Abdur Rahman, Amir of Afghanistan*. Trans. and ed. Mahomed Khan. Volume I. London: J. Murray, 1900. *Google Books*. Web. Last accessed June 28, 2012.

Barfield, Thomas. *Afghanistan: A Cultural and Political History*. Princeton: Princeton University Press, 2010.

Burton, Antoinette, ed. *The First Anglo-Afghan Wars. A Reader*. Durham: Duke University Press, 2014.

Dupree, Louis. *Afghanistan*. Princeton: Princeton University Press, 1980.

Ewans, Martin. *Afghanistan: A Short History of Its People and Politics*. New York: HarperCollins, 2002.

"Ex-Ammer's Death: A Link with Lord Roberts." *The Times* (London, England), November 16, 1923: 13. *Times Digital Archive*. Web. Last accessed July 24, 2015.

Henty, G. A. *For Name and Fame, or through Afghan Passes*. Blackie & Son, 1886. *Google Books*. Web. Last accessed January 5, 2009.

O'Ballance, Edgar. *Afghan Wars: Battles in a Hostile Land: 1839 to the Present*. Oxford: Oxford University Press, 2003.

"The Cabul Mutiny." *Blackwood's Edinburgh Magazine* 126, 126 (October 1879): 494–510. *Google Books*. Web. Last accessed October 29, 2015.

"The Ex-Amir Yakub Khan: From the Note-Book of a Staff Officer." *Blackwood's Edinburgh Magazine* 127, 776 (June 1880): 757–767. *ProQuest*. Web. Last accessed July 24, 2015.

Y is also for . . .

Yemen
Young Ireland
Yugantar Party
Yusufzais

Z is for Zam-Zammah

The cannon that inaugurates Rudyard Kipling's Kim evokes all the boyish derring-do at the heart of Victoria's empire. In this image from 1946, two boys play on the Zam-Zammah in the courtyard of the Prince Albert Memorial Museum in Lahore. Photo by Margaret Bourke-White, the LIFE Picture Collection.

Rudyard Kipling's 1901 novel *Kim* opens with the following famous passage:

> He sat, in defiance of multiple orders, astride the gun Zam-Zammah on her brick platform opposite the old Ajaib-Gher—the Wonder

House, as the natives call the Lahore Museum. Who hold Zam-Zammah, that "fire-breathing dragon," hold the Punjab, for the great green-bronze piece is always first of the conqueror's loot. There was some justification for Kim—he had kicked Lala Dinatanah's boy off the trunnions—since the English held the Punjab and Kim was English.

Published in the last year of Queen Victoria's reign, the novel is practically synonymous with Kipling's career as chronicler, and avatar, of nineteenth-century British imperialism. He had had the idea for the book for more than a decade before and had begun to sketch out a version of it in an unfinished manuscript called "Mother Maturin," which featured a half-caste Irish keeper of an opium den in Lahore (Sullivan, vii). Like Bankim Chandra's *Anandamath* (see **V is for "Vande Mataram"**), *Kim* was serialized, first in the New York monthly *McClure's Magazine* in the fall of 1900 and quickly thereafter in *Cassell's Magazine* in Britain. It appeared just as the British electorate was gearing up for the "Khaki election," the final general election of Victoria's reign. That proved a decisive victory for the Conservative Party, which firmly believed it was winning the then-raging Boer War.

The Zam-Zammah represents the hardware of conquest, though its origins predate the high noon of the Raj. Said to be commissioned by Ahmed Shah Durrani, the founder of the Durrani empire of Afghanistan in 1757, Zam-Zammah is part of the long history of the Great Game that helped to shape British colonial policy in India right down to Kipling's time (see **A is for Afghan Wars**). The gun's battle life was rooted in the eighteenth-century wars in and for the Punjab— so much so that the Lion of the Punjab, Ranjit Singh, considered it a real trophy as well as a good luck charm. After being badly damaged in the siege of Multan (1818), it was brought to Lahore where it was moved around and eventually found its place where Kim finds it—

which just happens to be in front of the Lahore museum where Kipling's father Lockwood was curator for several decades.

In the making of Kipling's *Kim*, the Zam-Zammah plays an important role, identifying him with the conquering race and reminding readers that the British are successors to the Mughals and the Hindus as rulers of India. In this scene, he vies with playmates for a place atop the gun:

> "Off! Off! Let me up!" cried Abdullah, climbing up Zam-Zammah's wheel.
>
> "Thy father was a pastry-cook, Thy mother stole the ghi," sang Kim. "All Mussulmans fell off Zam-Zammah long ago!"
>
> "Let me up!" shrilled little Chota Lal in his gilt embroidered cap. . . .
>
> "The Hindus fell off Zam-Zammah too. The Mussulmans pushed them off."

Here, the confidence that opened the novel is arguably somewhat muted, as Kim's friends try to challenge his status as king of the castle atop the Zam-Zammah. To be sure, Kipling's potted history is a confident assertion of Britain's military supremacy: The British are the most recent, and the undisputed, conquerors of India. Like him, they are on top. But will they be the last? If Hindus and Muslims can be pushed or fall off the pedestal, what guarantees a timeless Raj? Kim bests his buddies and his charisma carries him, and the plot, through the highways and byways of the Grand Trunk Road and beyond.

Thanks to Kipling's *Kim*, the Zam-Zammah is iconic. It represents the physical force, the threat of violence, that guaranteed the pleasurable romp through India that readers have loved—for its *Boys' Own* adventure spirit—and hated—for its careless attitude toward colonial subjugation. In the end, then, Kipling's gun really is the last word on Victorian imperialism.

Suggestions for Further Reading

Said, Edward. *Culture and Imperialism*. New York: Vintage Books, 1994.

Sharpe, Jenny. *Allegories of Empire: The Figure of Woman in the Colonial Text*. Minneapolis: University of Minnesota Press, 1993.

Suleri, Sara. *The Rhetoric of English India*. Chicago: University of Chicago Press, 1992.

Sullivan, Zohreh, ed. *Rudyard Kipling's* Kim: *A Norton Critical Edition*. New York: W. W. Norton, 2002.

Z is also for . . .

Zambesi
Zamindar
Zoning of prostitution
Zulu War

How to Teach this Book

Our hope is that this *ABC* will serve as a guide to students seeking both a grounding in the people and events that made imperialism what it was in the Victorian context *and* a set of pathways into the complexities of narrating Victoria's empire. This book can be read from *A* to *Z*, serving as a required text in any course on nineteenth-century British history, literature or cultural studies. It can also be used as a supplement to almost any text or syllabus in those courses. Instructors can direct students to specific entries that complement, or alternatively disrupt, the histories they find in their textbooks or novels or artifacts from the period. Linked to each letter is an image that makes all kinds of conversation possible as well. Discussion might include the extent to which the visuals reflect the content of the entries or point to other interpretive possibilities. And, of course, in each case, both the letter and the image open up horizons for alternative ABCs.

To that end, at the conclusion of every entry we have suggested a few other events or individuals that could be attached to each letter. One course assignment, therefore, could be for students to construct their own *ABC of Empire*. Ideally, this would be done collaboratively, with debate about how to shape the primer, what to include and what the key elements of the process should be. We would encourage instructors to structure that assignment so as to assure that students write some kind of introduction to their ABC. That way, the framing devices they have chosen are both acknowledged and clearly stated. For the ABC is not simply a random catalog. It is a form of argument about how to narrate, apprehend and otherwise engage with legacies of imperial power and violence—and how to materialize the rifts and fissures and resistances that empire provoked at every turn. Student ABCs will likely need a subtitle beyond the "ABC" as well. Subtitles tell readers what to expect thematically, temporally, geographically. In this case, the subtitle requires students to consider carefully how to align the individual letters with the larger arguments they are seeking to make about the character of Victorian imperialism.

Wherever possible, we have pointed to links and parallels and echoes among "letters" by referring to other relevant entries parenthetically. So, in "Kīngitanga," we point to **N is for Native Claim-making**; in "Dagga," we point to **O is for Opium**. This allows readers to see thematic connections across disparate geographies and historical events. These directionals could be used to guide students on how to write a narrative of disruption and dissent that draws selectively and schematically on multiple imperial spaces, helping them to plot the constancy of local challenge and imperial response. They might also literally map each letter by taking any nineteenth-century cartographic representation of empire and pinning it—with Gandhi, Riel, Convict Women, Hosay and Xhosaland—accordingly. The virtual/digital possibilities for this are limitless, even for those with minimal technological skills: wiki platforms or the interactive software program Prezi would work in intriguing ways to help visualize the rough terrain of resistance and instability that undergirds the ABC.

This *ABC of Victoria's Empire* reminds us that the possibilities for the creation of new narratives, if not also new knowledge, about the imperialism are legion. Q might be for Queensland here, but surely Queen Victoria herself also merits attention? If *J* were not for jihad, how would the ABC capture the significant challenges that Muslim fighters posed to the Northwest Frontier across the century? And if *B* is for Bold Fenian Men, how will women, Irish or otherwise, be represented? What is missing from this primer and how would the distribution of letters differently rebalance those absences in any reframing? And—the great challenge—what other items beyond Xhosaland can *X* conjure? Xanadu, from Samuel Taylor Coleridge's poem "Kubla Khan," is one possibility. It is technically pre-Victorian, but its links with opium smoking make it a possible candidate. Malcolm X, though clearly a twentieth-century figure, drew on anticolonial thinking and histories; a case could be made for his connection to a long line of antiracist agitation in the West. If these don't suit, what other *X*s should mark the spot?

Readers have the opportunity, then, to encounter and remake this book according to their own lights. In that sense, the ABC genre is very pliable; it models the flexibility of historical narrative and invites everyone to take up the possibilities of the craft. So take up the challenge and dive in.

Index